About the Author

Dr Richard G. Lewis FCIM is one of the Internet's leading consultants and authors, specializing in e-commerce, buyer psychology and marketing.

Over the last twelve years he has designed or developed over seventy e-commerce projects, many of which are now leaders in their market sector.

Richard has degrees in both business and computing, and holds a doctorate in e-commerce. He has over twenty five years experience of managing small businesses in the marketing, retail, service, and e-commerce sectors.

Richard has also written numerous research papers and books, including the bestseller, "The Small Business Guide to the Internet" (1999).

He is currently designing and developing websites for various high profile clients in the retail and Internet solutions sectors. Richard is available for consultancy work by contacting him through his website www.riskeliminator.com

Pre Cursor

All the Legal, Technical and Practical Short Cuts and Trade Secrets
You Need to Know *Before* Starting Your E-Commerce Empire

Dr Richard G. Lewis

Riana Publishing
International

Published by *Riana Publishing (International)*
A division of The Riana Group

A catalogue record of this book is
available from the British Library.

ISBN 13 978-0-9558640-2-5

Requests for permission should be directed to:

Riana Publishing (International)
Head Office
204 Sheikha Fatima Building
24 Street,
Hor Al Anz
P.O. Box 98393
Dubai
United Arab Emirates

publishing@rianagroup.com

DEDICATIONS

This book is dedicated to the memory of my father, Colin.

Special thanks to my wife Ana and my son David who make all my hard work worthwhile.

Preface

Thank you for choosing this book. This is a precise, step-by-step guide to absolutely everything you should know about the equipment, software, costs and legal requirements to set up and run a successful online business for under $1,000.

I sincerely believe that if you follow my advice you'll significantly reduce the risk associated with starting a successful online business and lay the solid foundations to building your e-commerce empire.

The purpose of this book is to help you:

1. **Reduce the Costs and Eliminate the Risk Associated With Starting Any Online Business.**

2. **Avoid the Common Pitfalls of Starting and Maintaining an Online Business.**

To further help ensure your success, I have provided various downloadable documents, advice and business tools that are relevant to starting an e-commerce project on the website www.riskeliminator.com

Good Luck!

Dr Richard G. Lewis FCIM

* All the prices and facts quoted in this book were correct at the time of going to press.

PARTS OF THIS BOOK

This book is a comprehensive and detailed guide to set up and run a successful online business for just $987 or less. It outlines all the necessary equipment, software and budget you'll need, as well as your legal and financial requirements.

PART ONE: HOW TO SET UP AN INTERNET BUSINESS

In this section I'll explain, in precise detail, absolutely everything you'll need to know about the equipment, software and connections you'll need, as well as accurately calculating the budget you'll require to set up and run a successful online business.

PART TWO: HOW TO FORM A COMPANY

Here you'll learn everything you'll need to know about the financial and legal requirements to setting up and running a successful online business.

Note: For advice on what to sell online, and how to sell it, read *Fortune Cookie* by Dr Richard G. Lewis, available from the website www.riskeliminator.com, along with other books in the *Competitive Advantage Series*.

This Book is Sponsored by:

For help with your
digital library conversion

phone: 888 CDS-2MP3
email: info@moondogdigital.com
web: www.moondogdigital.com
We rip, you rock!

CONTENT

Part One
How to Set Up an Internet Business

Part Two
How to Form a Company

Part One

How to Set Up an Internet Business

This comprehensive and detailed book explains exactly how to set up a business online, including everything you'll need to do, buy or organize. Everything you learn in this book will help you: whether you are just getting started or are already established online; whether you are sole trader, an owner-manager with a few employees, or a larger business with several employees.

Opportunity of a Lifetime

The Internet provides the greatest opportunity to make money that mankind has ever witnessed. We are still at the dawn of a new technological and economic age; the competitive advantage over the generations to come is incredible – this really is the chance of a lifetime! For the first time in history a sole trader working out of their back bedroom can compete with huge brands and be as profitable!

As a small business owner you now have access to a potential customer base of 1 billion people. Even if you sell to 1% of 1% of those people you will become rich! And you can now sell 24/7 – making money while you sleep. You can even run your online business from your smart phone!

Why Go Online?

Let's look into the future... Soon, to recoup the money they used to save the economy from the recent 'credit crunch', governments will increasingly tax individuals but not businesses; they will rely on businesses to generate revenue and jobs in the future. The only tax breaks and benefits will be for businesses not individuals. Also, to stimulate the economy, governments will provide more incentives for business start ups and employers.

Unemployment will continue to rise and the quality of jobs will decline as fewer top jobs are created and those with good jobs will keep them longer, so as to safe guard their income, savings, pensions etc. Because companies can pick and choose, salaries will continue to decrease and employees will be expected to take on more responsibilities, work harder and longer hours.

That's why having a successful Internet-based business may be your best insurance against the future - because it can increase your income and reduces your debt (estimated at $29,000 for each and every individual in the US alone). In fact, the benefits of going online are numerous, including:

- Huge potential customer audience (over 1 billion by 2010)
- Over $300 billion a year spent online by 2010 (USA alone)
- Broadband take up (500 million subscribers by 2010)
- Make money while you sleep; 24/7/365 customer access
- Global exposure; easily found by potential customers
- Be your own boss; shorter, flexible hours, better lifestyle, home or mobile office, work as and when you like
- Low start up (under $1,000), overhead or running costs
- Lower overhead, acquisition and operational costs result in higher profit margins

- Low risk – due to lower investment costs and accurate prelaunch market research and product testing
- Worldwide delivery, international virtual offices, and global telephone re-direction allow you to set up office anywhere in the world (and eliminate many tax liabilities)
- Launch your e-business while still in your full-time job
- Low difficulty; no technical expertise required
- Appear as big and professional as any global brand
- Cheaper, more powerful and efficient technology, constantly improve online facilities, software and security
- Attracting only a tiny percentage of the global audience will ensure you of a huge and constant income stream
- Every facet of your e-business model can be outsourced
- Pay-as-you-go technical, marketing and merchandizing services reduce operational costs, resources and risk
- Online outsourcing allows you to tap into a huge pool of the highest skills sets at the lowest prices in the world
- Update products, services and information instantly
- Immediate stock updates - no expensive catalogue reprints
- Easy creation of proprietary digital products and software
- Cost-free, automated, instant delivery of digital goods
- Easily target, dominate and service online niche markets
- Precise market placement through incredibly accurate market research and easy competitor analysis
- Highly targeted, cost-effective marketing (e.g. SEO or PPC)
- Email marketing campaigns ensure a high ROI
- Cheaper, faster shipping to worldwide destinations
- Higher targeted and individualized customer messages
- Better customer service e.g. FAQs assure customers pre-sale. Instant messaging or 'live' chat provides an instant response and improved customer satisfaction
- Promotion of products through detailed video presentations, 3D modeling and detailed graphics to demonstrate the benefits and features of products etc.

- Automated shopping carts, accounting and payroll programs reduce overheads, staff and mistakes
- Fast, secure and efficient online credit card processing
- No 'middleman'; reducing costs, admin and delivery times
- Real-time databases of members/clients, inventory and suppliers can be updated automatically, allowing business efficiency tools (e.g. Just-In-Time stock control) to be used
- Sourcing stock, manufacturers or suppliers is significantly more cost-effective, more efficient, simpler and easier
- Because website-based businesses can be fully-automated operations, business owners have considerably more time to develop their products, services, marketing and growth
- Brand expansion is faster, easier, and less costly
- Every new technology is a new business opportunity

Other benefits of going online include significant reductions in your marketing, sales and operational costs, extremely accurate conversion analysis, as well as reinforcing your company's profile and product or service brand to a huge global audience.

Any Room Left?

There are currently over 6 million small businesses in the United States. Based on what you hear in the news and by talking with others, you might assume that every business also has a website, right? Well, the truth is that a recent survey estimated that 67.8% of small businesses in the U.S. don't sell any products or services on the web. These small businesses are missing out on $1,000s. What an opportunity for you to steal a market!

Before you take advantage of this incredible opportunity and get online, you should first consider the hardware, software and financial investment you'll need to get started. You will also need to know your budget and legal requirements. Don't worry, this book will teach you EVERYTHING you'll need to know.

1

Equipment

To begin, you will need the proper equipment. There are three essential pieces of equipment required:

1. A **computer**, including peripherals such as a monitor, printing, scanner, etc.

2. A **modem** to connect your computer to a telephone line and/or an *Ethernet* connection

3. An **Internet connection** through a telephone jack, such as a digital subscriber line e.g. DSL, cable line, or satellite

Computers

To access the web, and to run all the necessary applications you will require to run a website, a computer should have at the minimum:

Hard drive: 80 Gigabytes (GB)
Memory: 1 GB RAM
Processor Speed: 1.8 Gigahertz (GHz)

Drives: DVD 16X
Modem: 56K
Monitor: 15 inch CRT (flat panel LCD best)
Networking: Ethernet LAN port on the system board

CRT stands for *cathode ray tube* describing the technology inside a traditional computer monitor or television set. A CRT monitor or TV is readily recognizable by its bulky form. LCD monitors and plasma television sets, that are referred to as *flat panel* displays, use different technologies than a CRT; allowing a much slimmer product profile.

When you purchase a computer, you are likely to receive a keyboard, mouse, and monitor as part of the package. Most desktop computer systems sold now by default come with LCD monitors. Because an LCD uses a matrix of cells to display its image, it has a fixed (or *native*) resolution at which it looks best.

A 15-inch LCD has a native resolution of 1024 x 768, while a 17- or 18-inch model will look its best at 1280 x 1024 or 1440 x 900 depending on the screen's format. If you set the monitor to a lower resolution the image will blur because the display will use only a portion of the pixels it contains and will scale up the resulting image to fill the screen. For most users, a 15-inch LCD monitor makes a good choice.

Three important things that will affect a computer's ability to help you move around effectively online are:

1. Processor Speed/Clock Speed
2. Quantity of RAM
3. Size of Hard Drive

Note: Some CRTs come with a *flat screen*, but this is not to be confused with a flat panel display.

PROCESSOR SPEED/CLOCK SPEED

In advertisements, you'll read about Pentium machines running at 2.5 gigahertz – but what does that mean?

Processors perform instructions under a time frame, or *cycle*. These cycles are measured in megahertz, or millions of cycles per second. This is known as *clock speed*. As processors become increasingly efficient, the time it takes to complete a cycle becomes shorter, and computers work faster and faster.

The megahertz is commonly used to express microprocessor clock speed. The megahertz, abbreviated MHz, is a unit of alternating current (AC) or electromagnetic (EM) wave frequency equal to one million hertz (1,000,000 Hz). Typical computer clock speeds, once on the order of a few hundred megahertz, are now often in the low gigahertz range. Often abbreviated *GHz*. 1 gigahertz = 1000 megahertz = a billion cycles per second.

What you really need to understand is that the bigger the number the faster the computer; a 2 GHz CPU, all else being equal, will calculate twice as fast as a 1 GHz CPU.

As processors become increasingly efficient they are able to process an increasing number of instructions and our computers – in conjunction with software – are seen as being capable of doing more and more sophisticated work faster.

QUANTITY OF RAM

RAM (Random Access Memory) is the amount of "processing space" your computer has to accomplish a computational task.

Measured in *megabytes* (or MBs), the more RAM you have, the better; RAM will affect the speed at which your different software can run, in addition to allowing you the option of running several software programs simultaneously. Also note that newer versions of system software and web browsers require more and more RAM.

SIZE OF HARD DRIVE

A *hard drive* is a mass storage device found in all PCs (with few exceptions) that is used to store permanent data such as the operating system, programs and user files. Hard drives come with many different storage capacities. Hard drive capacity is measured in *bytes* with common capacities being stated in MB (Megabytes) and GB (Gigabytes).

In the old days it was common to find hard drives with a capacity of just 5MB; nowadays it is hard to buy a new hard drive with less than 40GB, that's 40,960 Megabytes. Common hard drive capacities these days range from 40GB up to and exceeding 120GB.

As a real world example, let's take a color photo that takes up 500 KB of storage space on a hard drive. If you had a 40GB hard drive, you could potentially store up to 81,290 color photos. Although this is obviously hypothetical since your hard drive also stores your operating system and programs.

Note: Don't confuse the size of your hard drive with the amount of RAM in your machine. While both are measured in megabytes, your hard drive is primarily storage space; RAM is processing space.

Where to Buy

Using the Internet does not require a particularly powerful computer and can be accessed from any type of computer: a desktop, laptop, mobile phone, or even a hand-held PDA (personal digital assistant).

However, to get the fullest use of all the utilities available on the Internet, the computer you use should be the fastest you can afford. The faster your computer the lower your overall costs for using the Internet will be. Naturally, your budget will play an important part in your decision-making, but the fastest machine you can afford may save you considerable cost in the long term.

When it comes to buying a computer for your business, the options range from either purchasing it directly from a major manufacturer, retailer, mail order or online company. You can also find companies that assemble a system specifically for you with all necessary software pre-loaded.

There are advantages in purchasing from a well-known brand or a local supplier. Big brand manufacturers tend to be more expensive but provide support, after sales service, warranties etc., while local suppliers tend to give better value for money and a faster response to any problems.

Desktop computers, with the minimum stated requirements, start as low as $500, topping out at around $850. Laptops with these requirements start at $800 and can go as high as $2000.

Mac or a PC?

There are two main types of computer systems, a *Mac* and a *PC*. A Mac is manufactured by Apple and uses Mac software whereas a PC is made by such companies as Dell, IBM, or Compaq and uses Microsoft software. In order to determine whether you should purchase a Mac or a PC, you will need to decide what you want to do with your computer.

All computers will work well for the casual user. For instance, both a PC and a Mac work well for web browsing, document manipulation, scheduling and management, and multimedia playback. However, there are some platforms which excel in specific areas:

- Home Office. Newer versions of Microsoft's Office are not very compatible with the Mac computer. Therefore, if you are using these products, a PC would be a good choice.

- Content Creation. Although PCs use Adobe's multimedia content creation software, professionals who need to create studio-quality content will opt for Mac. The Mac has been long touted as an artist's choice.

Although Apple Mac was historically known as an easy-to-use platform with powerful multimedia applications, these are no longer Mac's primary strengths. Instead, the Mac's strengths are focused on an easy user interface with a variety of pre-installed software that gets even a novice up and running quickly. They also have excellent help, tuition and user support.

PCs, on the other hand, use Windows and businesses tend to use Windows because it's what they know, and what their schools, offices, and friends use. The strength of pre-built PCs is that you receive a pre-configured and pre-installed system that is ready to install most third-party applications and be compatible with a majority of other computers in existence.

There are weaknesses to both platforms as well. Mac's weakness is its price and its compatibility. Apple desktops and laptops are very expensive when compared to PCs. They are also very proprietary in regard to their hardware, software, and software licensing. This brings a higher cost of hardware and services, resulting in a higher ownership cost.

A PC's components such as power sources and motherboards can vary from manufacturer to manufacturer. For instance, manufacturers such as Dell and HP/Compaq will sell models that are very proprietary, yet others may adhere to component standards used throughout the PC industry. Also, Windows licensing has become extremely restrictive, with Vista and many peripheral devices (printers, scanners, etc.) that worked with older systems no longer work with a Vista-running computer.

Therefore, determining which computer platform is best for you depends on what you need to use the computer for. In general, for most businesses, unless a large amount of graphics work will be done, a PC will work well and is more cost-effective.

Peripherals

In addition to the computer and monitor, you will need to think about peripherals. The term *peripheral* is used to describe devices that are optional in nature, as opposed to hardware that is either demanded or always required. Apart from peripherals that come as standard with the computer, two that you will need to consider are a printer and a scanner.

PRINTERS

The most important consideration when purchasing a printer is the type of technology the printer uses to print. Today you will find two major types of technologies available: inkjet and laser. Inkjet printers are an affordable and effective solution for home businesses.

The cost of ink is a very important factor when purchasing a printer. If the printer becomes a frequently used device you may find that the price of the ink can far surpass the price of the printer. Therefore, consider how much the printer's ink will cost when it needs to be replaced. Also, consider how often the cartridge will have to be replaced (i.e. 'pages per cartridge') and check if the printer accepts separate color cartridges.

The color printing process works by mixing four color inks, magenta, cyan, yellow and black in varying amounts to create all the colors required. Some printers use a separate cartridge for each color and black.

Other printers use one cartridge with three separate compartments holding each color (c,m,y). Black always comes as a separate cartridge. Some manufacturers may include all the color inks in a single cartridge, forcing you to have to purchase a whole cartridge when only one color needs replacing.

In addition, see if the cartridges are just ink or ink and nozzles. Cartridges with ink and nozzles will cost more than those that have just ink.

The price range can vary depending upon the quality of the printer and the type of printer. Below is a price range of what to expect when purchasing a printer. Most inkjet printers cost between $40 and $400, though many pre-packaged computer systems now come with printers.

With a laser printer the light source is a laser. Laser printers quickly became popular due to the high quality of their print and their relatively low running costs. Output quality has improved, with 600dpi resolution becoming more standard, and build has become smaller, making them more suited to small business use.

Laser printers have a number of advantages over inkjet technology. They produce much better quality black text documents than inkjets, and they tend to be designed more for the long haul - that is, they turn out more pages per month at a lower cost per page than inkjets. Another factor of importance to the business user is that the handling of envelopes, card and other non-regular media is easier than with an inkjet printer. Laser printers also cost between $40 and $400.

SCANNERS

Most companies need scanners, mainly to digitize documents. Doing so will help you secure and manage crucial information such as tax returns. Additionally, most scanners offer a technology called *OCR* (optical character recognition), which converts clear, high-contrast printed documents into text files you can edit in a word processing program instead of having to retype all the information into a word processing document.

Many companies opt for a flatbed scanner as opposed to a sheet-fed scanner. With a flatbed model, you can scan materials and three-dimensional objects other than paper. With a flatbed, material of reasonable thickness and just about any size can be scanned without fear of jamming the mechanism or losing something in the mechanism of the machine.

In some cases, a sheet-fed scanner is right for you. Here's one good reason: it takes up less space. A sheet-fed scanner takes up only a fraction of the area used by a flatbed scanner on your desktop. In fact, many sheet-fed models are portable enough to be used on the road with a laptop computer.

The more dots per inch (dpi) you can scan, the better. For most users, a 1200 x 2400 DPI scanner is sufficient. Only if you are doing design and graphic art applications will you need anything higher.

You will also want to look at bit depth. Again, the higher the bit depth, the better the scanner; if you're buying a new scanner, stick with a scanner that offers at least 36-bit color. Anything more than 36-bit is usually overkill for a typical small business owner.

Both flatbed and sheet-fed scanners start around $35 and can go as high as several thousand dollars. For your purposes, one in the lower ranges will more than suffice.

DIGITAL CAMERA

Though not truly a peripheral, having a digital camera can help sell your products for higher prices because a good quality photo will make your product look better to the public. They can also help cut down on the number of questions from potential buyers because they will be able to see all the details of your product, especially if you have views from many different angles.

Since you will be dealing with the Internet, super-high mega-pixels aren't an absolute necessity. But you still might want to look into a higher-resolution camera if you need to capture very fine details.

A digital camera's *megapixel* count is an important specification. Stating the number of megapixels is another way of expressing a camera's *resolution* - the higher the megapixel number, the higher the resolution. In general, higher-resolution cameras let you produce larger, higher-quality digital images and prints.

If you're interested in producing mostly small snapshots or images to send via email or publish on the web, you probably don't need anything better than a 5-megapixel camera, as images with greater definition than this will require a file size that will be impractical because they will not download in a reasonable time.

Another specification you need to consider is the *focal range*. Cameras with greater focal range can zoom out to fit more into a shot or zoom in to fill the frame with the subject. Optical zoom produces sharper images than digital zoom. All new point-and-shoot and advanced cameras offer at least a 3X zoom that will work sufficiently for most online business needs.

You can ask yourself these four questions to help determine the digital camera that is best for you:

1. *Will you need to be taking close-up pictures of small objects that require a lot of detail to sell on your website?*

All cameras let you take close-up photos, but some are easier than others. If you're going to be doing a lot of close-up work, look for a camera with an easy-to-use close-up feature.

2. *Will you be taking photos from far off?*

If so, you will need a camera with higher optical zoom. Most offer 3X zoom, capturing a picture 3 times larger than if you were seeing it with the naked eye. For far away photos, you will want an optical zoom that is more than a 3X. Keep in mind that cameras with a bigger zoom are usually heavier and bulkier because of the size of the lens.

3. *What about LCD size?*

The *LCD* [Liquid Crystal Display] is what makes a digital camera unique because you can see the photo you just took and decide if it truly captured the image correctly. A large LCD will show the details more clearly; however, it will also be larger and drain the batteries more quickly.

4. *Are you on a budget?*

You can buy a perfectly good 5-megapixel name-brand camera with lots of features starting as low as $40. The important thing is to find the camera that offers the features you need at the best price. Often, the best price comes from buying online; however, try out different cameras in a store before buying so that you absolutely understand the different features of each camera.

Below is a chart to help you determine which features are right for you.

Feature	Very Important	Somewhat Important	Not Important
High Optical Zoom (4x or greater)			
Larger LCD (greater than one inch)			
Wide-Angle Lens			
Pocket Size or Lightweight			
4-to-5 megapixels			
6 or more megapixels			
$350 or less			
Extra Memory			
Memory Card Reader			

Almost all digital cameras come with software that lets you download images to your PC and print them. Some cameras even come with picture-editing software, but it will be important to have a higher quality photo-editing application for most businesses.

Modems or Ethernet Card

The only other hardware required will be an internal or external modem or an Ethernet card. A *modem* is used when you choose a dial-up connection for your computer and connects your computer, via a modem cable, to your phone jack. It converts data from a computer into sound signals that can then be transmitted over a normal telephone line. It works the opposite way around when receiving information. Your modem should be at least 56Kbps.

If you use a DSL line, a cable connection, or wireless connection to connect to the Internet, you will need an *Ethernet card*. These days most of the computers come with built-in Ethernet cards, and unless specified, you won't need to install one. An Ethernet card is hundreds of times faster than a modem and can make your work output much faster and cost-effective.

2

Internet Connection

As would be expected, the capacity and speed of the basic connection service will determine the cost of your Internet access. The general rule is that the higher the bandwidth capacity and the faster the speed, the higher the cost to install and maintain your Internet link.

There are several ways of connecting to the Internet: from a simple dial-up link using a standard telephone line to faster and "always on" connections using a leased line, ISDN, ADSL, 'cable', satellite, terrestrial fixed and mobile wireless. The faster the connection the greater its capacity, enabling the fast transfer and download of data across the Internet.

The type of connection you use also has a direct effect on the speed with which you will be able to use the Internet. The capacity of an Internet connection is referred to as its *bandwidth*, and is measured in bits of data per second, a bit being an on or off 1 or 0 signal. A thousand bits is a Kilobit (Kb), a million bits is a Megabit (Mb), a thousand million bits is a Gigabit (Gb) etc. However, data files are measured in Bytes, KiloBytes (KB), etc, with a Byte calculated as eight bits.

So, a 1MB file is 8,000,000 bits and, in theory, will take 200 seconds (3 minutes 20 seconds) to transfer over a perfect 40kb/s (40,000 bits per second) connection.

Although there are many ways to connect to the Internet, they vary mainly by connection and by speed. A connection may be one that has to be launched each time you wish to use it, or you can have an "always-on" connection, also known as a *broadband* connection. The first is connected by a modem and the second through an Ethernet card.

Speed, the second variable, determines how quickly you can receive and send data to and from your computer.

Pros and Cons of Different Internet Connections

Method	Pros	Cons
Dial-up	Inexpensive	Slower than broadband
	Available anywhere	Can incur local phone charges
	Can connect using a cell phone and a cell phone modem	Needs two lines to make phone calls while online
Broadband	Much faster than dial-up	More expensive than dial-up
	Always on; no delay to connect	Not available in all areas
	Doesn't need two lines to make phone calls while online	
Wireless	You can be connected to the Internet almost anywhere	Connection is less secure
	No extra wiring to connect more employees to the Internet	Signal can be lost for a variety of reasons – even a microwave oven
	Doesn't need two lines to make phone calls while online	Slower than broadband

High rates of transfer are said to be "fast" connections or "high speed" connections.

Many companies choose to have an "always-on" connection because of the speed, even though such a connection can be a bit more costly.

Finding an Internet Service Provider (ISP)

Internet service providers (ISPs) are companies that provide dial-up or broadband Internet connections, usually for a monthly fee.

DIAL-UP

Earthlink, NetZero/Juno, BasicISP, People PC and AOL are some of the most popular dial-up services. They charge anywhere from $9.95 to $24.95 per month. The difference in fees reflects the different services each company offers. For instance, the companies that offer more comprehensive customer service or tech support charge more.

BROADBAND

Broadband service is mainly available in three different ways:

1. **Cable modem:** Uses the same connection that delivers cable TV. A cable Internet connection is fast and reliable but not available in all areas.

2. **DSL (digital subscriber line):** Uses your existing phone line but doesn't tie up the line. In other words, you can make phone calls while connected to the Internet. However, DSL often requires installation fees and the farther you are from the provider the more likely it is that your speed will be slower.

3. **Satellite:** Available where cable and DSL aren't. As long as you have a clear view of the southern sky, you can receive this service. However, satellite is slower than both cable and DSL, can be interrupted by bad weather, and requires the installation of a satellite dish on your house or in your yard.

When it comes to choosing a broadband service, find out what's available:

- Contact the cable TV provider in your area and see if they also provide an Internet service.

- Call your local phone company to inquire about DSL. If they offer DSL, find out your distance from the DSL transmission location.

- If cable and DSL are not options, research the major satellite TV services. They probably also offer an Internet service in your area.

- Find out which additional services the providers offer, such as email accounts and spam blocking.

- Compare speeds of various services. Decide whether the extra speed is worth the extra cost.

- Compare prices. Be sure to include setup costs, equipment, and installation costs, if any.

WIRELESS

In addition to broadband and dial-up services, web users are now able to connect to the Internet wirelessly, accessing the web without wires or cables of any type.

Wireless technology allows users to have mobile connections, accessing the web (with some limitations) where and when they need to. This can be accomplished via public hot spots (designated areas that offer wireless), cell phones and new USB Modems. Wireless connections allow users to connect whether they are at home, school, work, or on the road.

Ongoing Costs

When considering dial-up connections, some companies will charge you fees on a monthly basis; others on an annual basis. Some charge you per minute, based on the length of your connection time. Generally, you are charged lower fees if you pay annually in advance. Those that charge you per minute can work out to be more expensive.

There is a tendency for companies to underestimate the amount of time they will be connected to the Internet. Therefore, if you budget for a particular amount of Internet-related charges based on the "per minute" charge, you could end up paying considerably more, often more than would have been the case with monthly or annual billing.

For broadband connections, you will typically have a monthly fee. Be aware that you may be offered a special rate for the first 3, 6, or 12 months. Once that period is over, the rate will return to normal. Find out what the normal rate is going to be before determining if you can afford the cost of broadband.

User Support

The issue of service backup, should anything go wrong, is something that is rarely thought of until it is too late. An ISP should constantly monitor its network's performance and have contingency plans in place for network outages. It should have built-in redundancy (spare capacity in the event of an emergency), and on-website backups for its servers.

Backup generators should also be in place in case of power failure, and generators should keep any necessary equipment functioning for a reasonable time. An ISP should be able to cope with any service failure and preferably have a backup Network Operations Centre (NOC).

In order to remain competitive, many ISPs have started to offer more substantial educational and training programs, customized security arrangements, and other services tailored for business customers, as part of their user support facilities.

Training can be especially important for organizations without the facilities, resources and cash for in-house training programs as training and maintenance can represent the highest costs of an Internet presence. It is in the interest of every business to talk to several potential providers before making a decision about an Internet connection.

You should ask potential ISPs what kinds of user support they provide. For example, in addition to training, having online user help can be very useful. You may have to pay higher ongoing fees for higher levels of support, so you need to balance your finances with your requirements.

Checklist for Choosing a Service Provider

Selecting an Internet service provider and determining the most appropriate Internet connection to support your particular business objectives should involve a consideration of all the options available. It may help if you use a checklist with each ISP before you decide on which would be the most beneficial and appropriate to your specific business needs.

ISP Checklist

1. Does the ISP provide the kind of connection you want (dial-up, DSL, etc)?

2. Which kinds of service does the ISP provide in your local area?

3. What level of technical support is available from the ISP — Web or email only, or can you call for support?

4. Does the ISP provide software for connecting to the Internet? Most companies provide this for free, but check this before signing up.

5. Check the ISP's reliability rating with your area's *Better Business Bureau* before you do business with them.

Training

If your Internet-based venture is going to succeed, you may require staff that will need to be trained. This may sound obvious but a recent report revealed that a quarter of all e-commerce ventures fail due to lack of understanding and support.

Surveys show that between North American and Europe's largest corporations, almost a quarter of e-commerce projects are abandoned before completion. For most, failure is not simply a result of a lack of investment but a lack of appropriate planning.

As important as the money spent on the software, the equipment, the network links, and the staff necessary to get a website up and running, is the need for information on the website being kept up-to-date.

If the company is presenting its product or service range or price list on the web, it is essential that the website be updated regularly with current and accurate prices and products. Any staff and equipment should be budgeted to carry out the updates and maintenance of the website.

The right staff, the right suppliers and the right set of hardware and software, which has a sensible upgrade path, is the prerequisites of a cost-effective and competitive website presence.

All these elements could be coordinated to within a specific strategic plan and development time span. For a single owner-manager these elements are much more difficult to co-ordinate and maintain.

3

Security Issues

In the last 10 years, the availability of the Internet has allowed even small businesses to have customers all over the world and even have offices in different locations throughout the world. However, with this growth and connectivity comes a major problem – computer security.

Despite the very best people working on network security, the last few years has seen an increasing number of hackers and criminals that infiltrate computers and systems. For each security breach that is controlled, a new and even more vicious one is developed.

Why are these security threats so successful? In general, employees of companies don't understand how the different network security threats work and often do not know that new threats exist. In the following paragraphs, you will learn about the 10 biggest and most dangerous threats to your small business computer security and how to ward off these attacks.

Viruses and Worms

Most people assume that a *virus* is any kind of computer threat. Actually, it is *malware* that inserts a code into a document or program and then, like a medical virus, spreads itself through your computer by various means.

Viruses were the original type of malware. Today, viruses are still the most common type of computer threat and most (90%) spread themselves through attachments on emails.

However, a virus cannot enter your computer unless you do something to allow it to do so. That is why it is important to train your employees to never open an attachment from someone they don't know or weren't expecting. Even if you know the sender, an attachment can contain a virus.

There is something else similar to a virus called a *worm*. The problem with worms is that they attach themselves to an email and not in an attachment. Simply reading the email will cause them to get into your computer and quickly spread.

Therefore, it should be a priority of every company and individual to use virus protection software to limit the incoming malware, and then to educate employees to make sure those worms and viruses that slip through never get opened. *Anti-virus programs* look at the contents of each file looking for specific patterns called a *virus signature*. Every virus signature will be removed or destroyed.

When the anti-virus program vendors learn about a new virus, they provide an updated set of virus signatures that include that new one. Through features provided by the updated anti-virus program, your computer also automatically learns of this new virus and begins checking each file for it, along with checking for all the older viruses.

Trojan Horses

A *Trojan horse* is a malware attack that disguises itself as something innocent, such as a computer game, or a YouTube search results page. A recent Trojan horse installed a keylogger onto the infected computer. This *keylogger* was used to record every *keystroke* by a computer's user, thus stealing financial account information and passwords.

Trojans are particularly dangerous because they all appear so safe. Trojans hide on websites, in free software, or in links sent via email.

Training employees to look for Trojan horses may not be useful because there are so many different types. Instead, you may want to do the following:

- Disallow users from downloading freeware

- Block links imbedded in emails

- Create a list of approved websites that employees may visit

Though these measures may sound drastic, computers infected with a Trojan horse often require a complete reformatting of the hard drive.

Spam

Most people believe that *spam* is unsolicited email. Spam is actually anonymous unsolicited email. In 2008, the number of spam messages increased 150% to 150 billion spam messages every day. That's 25 spams per day for every single person on earth, including children! And spam is becoming more dangerous each day.

In 2008, more than 83% of spam contained a URL to a rogue web server that was frequently serving malware, a program or file that is designed to specifically damage or disrupt a system. In fact, URL-based viruses increased 256%.

Spam email can be unsolicited email used to coordinate spam attacks, designed to take up so much bandwidth on a network so as to cause it to crash. A more recent trend is image spam, which eats up even more bandwidth and isn't caught by typical spam filters. Another brand new technique that spammers are using is called "news service" spam, which uses legitimate headlines to trick recipients into opening spam emails that are filled with unsolicited advertisements.

Most spam can be filtered out by a good email filter. In addition, you should require your employees to use separate email accounts for their personal Internet use, and demand that company email accounts not be used to sign up for any online service or freebie.

In addition, when creating company email accounts make sure to use a naming system which is not easily guessable (e.g. JSmith@domain.com), as spammers are increasingly going through common name lists in order to harvest emails to spam.

Phishing

Anyone who has ever used PayPal or does their banking online has probably received dozens of emails with titles such as, "URGENT: Update Account Status".

These emails are all attempts by a spammer to "phish" for your account information. *Phishing* refers to spam emails designed to trick recipients into clicking on a link to an unsecure website where they steal account information from sites such as eBay, PayPal, or even your bank.

A phishing email supplies you with a link to click on, which will take you to a page where you can re-enter all your account details, including credit card number(s) and/or passwords. Of course, these sites aren't the actual bank's website, even though they look like it.

Phishing is a huge and growing problem for business owners. To protect your network, it is vital that you educate your employees about the most common ways phishing occurs. A single phishing attack can compromise an entire network's security if the employee is tricked into giving his network account information.

You should use a sophisticated email filter to limit the number of phishing attacks. New Internet browsers, such as *Internet Explorer .8* and Mozilla's *Firefox 3.5* have built-in phishing filters, which should be left 'on'.

Packet Sniffers

Packet sniffers capture data streams over a network in order to capture usernames, passwords and credit card numbers. The result is the loss of data, trade secrets, or online account balances.

Packet sniffers work by monitoring and recording all the information that comes from and goes to your computer. In order to be effective, the packet sniffer must have access to the network you are using.

The most common way to do this is through using something called *honeypots*. Honeypots are unsecured WIFI access points that hackers set up and trap people into using. Typically, these honeypots are set up in public places such as airports, and the WIFI network is titled something like "Free Public Wi-Fi". Unsuspecting individuals sign on and the packet sniffer grabs their personal information when they enter things such as their credit card info into a website.

Education is the best way to deal with packet sniffers. Teach your employees to never access the Internet through an unsecured connection by installing a *firewall*. Also insist that your employees use a variety of sign on names and passwords for access.

A firewall is the guard that determines whether information intended for your computer should be allowed in or be stopped. Essentially, a firewall keeps unwanted traffic out and allows appropriate traffic to enter. To do this, the firewall has to look at every piece of information – every *packet* – that tries to enter or leave a computer. The firewall records several things: where the packet came from, where it is going, and when it was viewed.

Passwords are also very important. Each password your employees use should be unrelated to other passwords. They should never be written down or shared with other employees. You need to make sure the length and content of each password is strong.

For example, if a password allows 8 digits as well as letters and numbers, your employees should take advantage of these parameters instead of using only 5 numbers. Additionally, passwords should be changed often.

Maliciously-Coded Websites

Common forms of maliciously-coded websites are sites that appear to allow you to make donations to victims of natural disasters. You will find a sign-in page and then be asked to enter in your credit card number and other personal information.

To combat maliciously-coded websites, you should only purchase items from security certified sites and use PayPal instead of a credit card. Maliciously-coded websites typically do not accept PayPal payments since they are easier to trace than typical credit card payments. Additionally, your employees should never sign up for new *Web 2.0* applications (e.g. social networking websites) without using a different username and password than they ordinarily use for sensitive data. Finally, you will also need to keep your virus and email protections up to date.

Hardware Loss and Residual Data Fragments

Hardware loss is a large cause of the more than 10 million cases of identity theft suffered by Americans each year. Although not what most people think of as a network security threat, stolen laptops pose a huge threat to networks. Even sold or discarded computers and laptops can be a problem since businesses often sell older computers without completely wiping the drives clean of data, including system passwords.

You can minimize this threat easily by encrypting sensitive company data, especially data that is most likely to "leave the office" with employees carrying laptops. Despite the benefits of securing data, 64% of companies were more concerned about data loss than the cost of replacing hardware; however, only 12% were actually using encryption.

Additionally, you should wipe files on old hard drives before selling or discarding the computer, and develop a system to track employee hardware, such as smartphones, smart memory cards, and USB flash drives.

Zombie Computers and Botnets

A recent New York Times article estimates that as much as 80% of spam messages are sent out by the computers of ordinary individuals who have no idea their computers have been converted into 'zombies'.

A *zombie* computer is one infected with malware that silently sends out thousands of emails from the owner's email address.

Infected 'zombie' computers, are organized by spammers into small groups called *botnets*. The 'zombie' malware threat is expected to continue to grow both in number and variety over the next few years. Preventing 'zombies' is possible if your employees keep all their security software up to date and run virus scans daily. Additionally, train your employees to spot computer slowdowns or crashes as these may be signs that their computers have been infected.

Insider Attacks

Insider attacks are becoming an increasing threat nationwide. For many businesses it's not a question of "if, but when" a disgruntled or cash-motivated employee will attempt to disrupt the system or steal proprietary data and sell it on the black market.

The problem is that the applications used to keep outsiders from attacking computers, such as firewalls and security software, have made it easier for insider threats. The insider threat is always there because people on the inside are aware of what steps a company has taken to secure the network and the various applications used.

Ways to keep insider attacks from happening include *least-privilege access* and *two-factor authentication.*

1. The Law of Least Privilege: The law of least privilege allows people access only to those applications needed and only under the context in which they need it. The assumption is that any other access is for insider security risks.

2. Two-Factor Authentication: An authentication factor is a piece of information and process used to verify a person's identity. Two-factor authentication (T-FA) is a system where two different factors are used to authenticate to be even surer that the person using the system is truly who they say they are. Using more than one factor is sometimes called *strong authentication.*

Securing Software

Most vendors provide patches that are supposed to fix *bugs* in their products. Vendors often provide free patches on their websites. When you purchase programs, it's a good idea to see if and how the vendor supplies patches, and also if and how they provide a way to ask questions about their products.

You can receive patch notices through email by subscribing to mailing lists operated by the programs' vendors. Through this type of service, you can learn about problems with your computer even before you discover them and, hopefully, before intruders have the chance to exploit them.

Consult the vendor's website to see how to get email notices about patches as soon as they're available.

Information Security Management Systems

An *Information Security Management System* (ISMS) is a set of policies concerned with information management. The key concept of ISMS is for an organization to design, implement and maintain processes and systems for effectively managing information accessibility, thus ensuring the confidentiality, integrity and availability of information assets and minimizing information security risks. All training, implementation of anti-virus software, firewalls, and laptop safety policies fall under ISMS.

The best way to create and maintain an ISMS is to follow a "Plan-Do-Check-Act" policy. The 'plan' phase helps you determine what needs to be done, such as install a firewall or anti-virus program. The 'do' phase implements these controls. In other words, such software is installed. The 'check' phase allows you to review and evaluate these security measures to determine if they are effective. Finally, the 'act' phase allows you to make the necessary changes.

Items to Consider for an ISMS:

- Anti-Virus Software
- Firewalls
- Passwords
- Free software download policies
- Blocking email embedded links
- Email filters
- Separate work and personal email policies
- Email naming system policies
- Purchasing online policies
- Encryption
- Old hardware policies
- Updating programs with patches
- Authentication processes
- Privilege Access processes

Contingency Planning, Disaster and Data Recovery

No matter how tight your controls, there still may be a breach of security. Additionally, there are disasters beyond your control, such as fires, floods, or even simple power outages. Therefore, you will need a plan to recover data when such a disaster strikes.

The first step in coming up with a recovery plan is to list possible risks that could threaten your system and then rank them in the order of likelihood.

For instance, those computers in flood-prone areas may place flood damage higher on their list than someone with a business in an area that is prone to summer wild fires. You will also want to rank these possibilities according to impact.

For instance, the impact of a power outage may have a higher impact on your business than that of a hurricane threat; therefore, a power outage would be a higher priority in your disaster recovery plan.

Once you've figured out your risks, you must determine your budget. Keep in mind that preventative costs are typically far less than the cost of a disaster, should it happen. A good place to begin is to understand the cost of downtime to the business. How long can your business afford to be without its computer systems should one of your threats occur? Disaster recovery budgets vary from company to company but they typically run between 2% and 8% of the overall IT budget.

The recovery procedure should be written in a detailed plan or "script" with specific duties assigned to each member of your business. The script will also outline priorities for the recovery.

Once your procedures are set, you should test it frequently. This will validate that everything will work and allow you to address shortcomings. You will also want to re-evaluate your plan yearly to make sure that your plan still meets your growing business needs.

Obviously, one of the best things you can do to alleviate the problems of disaster recovery is to make backups of important files and folders. Firstly, you will need to determine:

- What files to back up? These should be files that are not easy to recreate or reinstall.

- How often should the backups occur? In the best case scenario, this should happen daily.

- Where should you back them up to? For instance, you can back up your files to a CD, a removable disk drive, or even an Internet service. Many Internet services, such as *Mozy* will allow you to back up files for free. If you have a large amount of files, you can access their service for less than $5 per month. Therefore, for less than $60 a year, you can have your files secured.

If you decide to store your files on disks or drives, be sure that they are stored in a secure location not prone to the same threats as the primary computer.

Networking

A *network* links two or more computer components together for the purpose of sharing data. Networks are built with a mix of computer hardware and computer software. Utilities such as the Internet, printers, scanners, and computers can be connected. A network lets you transfer files, pictures, and information without using any kind of disk or external drive. Most businesses decide to use a network because they have more than one computer and want to share information and computer components.

Taking time to configure the security features of your network is essential. Here are a few things you can do to protect your wireless network:

- **Secure your wireless router or access point administration interface**. This sounds fancy but all it means is to change the default password to your router as soon as you set it up.

- **Don't broadcast your network's name**. Most routers automatically and continually broadcast the network's name. This will make your network visible to **any** wireless systems within range of it. Turn off this broadcast, known as SSID, to make it invisible to passers-by.

- **Enable WPA encryption.** WPA is Wi-Fi Protected Access and it protects your passwords. It is built into Windows XP and other modern wireless operating systems.

- **Use Mac filtering.** If you use a Mac computer, you will need to use Mac filtering. Unlike Internet Protocol (IP) addresses, Mac addresses are unique to specific network adapters, so by turning on Mac filtering you can limit network access to only your systems.

Following these easy steps can ensure that no one intercepts your Wi-Fi traffic.

Intellectual Property

Another security issue is *intellectual property*. Patents, copyrights, trademarks and industrial designs, as well as know-how or trade secrets, are often collectively referred to as intellectual property (IP). Many firms have such property without even being aware of it or of the need to take measures to protect it.

PATENTS

A *patent* is a document, issued by the federal government, which grants to its owner a legally enforceable right to exclude others from practicing the invention described and claimed in the document. Congress has specified that a patent will be granted if the inventor files a timely application that adequately describes a new, useful and unobvious invention of proper subject matter.

Patents are obtained through a complex administrative proceeding in the United States Patent and Trademark Office. Since the legal rules that govern this proceeding are quite extensive and often complicated, it is strongly recommended that an inventor seek the assistance of an experienced patent attorney before beginning this process.

TRADEMARK

A *trademark* is a word, name, or symbol that is used in trade with goods to indicate the source of the goods and to distinguish them from the goods of others. A servicemark is the same as a trademark except that it identifies and distinguishes the source of a service rather than a product.

Trademark rights may be used to prevent others from using a confusingly similar mark, but not to prevent others from making the same goods or from selling the same goods or services under a clearly different mark.

COPYRIGHT

Copyright is a form of protection provided to the authors of "original works of authorship", including: literary, dramatic, musical, artistic, and certain other intellectual works whether or not they were published.

Unless you state otherwise, no one can make copies, even if they give you credit. The same holds true if you wish to use information. Unless you have permission or the work does not have a copyright, you may not use what is already written as your own.

Our world is becoming more and more intertwined as the Internet grows into an everyday network. Consequently, with such connectivity come many different security issues. It is imperative that business owners defend their networks and continue to educate themselves and their employees to keep security breaches to a minimum.

INDUSTRIAL DESIGN

An *industrial design* relates to the external appearance of a finished product. It is defined by the product's unique attributes, such as shape, contours, color, ornamentation, pattern, configuration, material and texture.

For instance, an industrial design can be a design on a vase to a font style and everything in between. Industrial designs are valuable intellectual property because creating them from scratch requires a great deal of investment in terms of money, resources and man-hours.

A unique design can add substantial commercial value to a product and increase its marketability. It also often becomes a recognizable brand of a particular manufacturer.

Once you have created an industrial design, you should get it registered in your name as soon as possible to protect it from unauthorized copying. This is because, unlike a copyright or trademark, you as a creator cannot claim legal proprietorship or protection of a design until you have got it formally registered in your name. Besides, it will lose novelty in one year or less after its disclosure in many jurisdictions.

Note: Intellectual Property protection and registration companies, such as www.ipprot.com, will help you protect your IP.

4

Software

Without software, your computer won't do anything. You must use software to make your computer run. Software will get your computer started and it will manipulate data on your computer.

Anything that can be stored electronically is *data*. *Software* is the programs that help you create, view and manipulate this data. The storage and display devices are *hardware*.

When you purchase a computer program, you are buying software. There are two main types of software: systems software and applications software. Systems software often comes already installed with the computer, or as a disk to be installed, and includes the operating system.

Applications software is programs that perform work for the user. This section will focus on various types of applications software.

Word Processing Software

Word processing is using your computer to create, edit, and print documents. This is the most used application for computer users. The best thing about word processing is that you can make changes to your document without retyping the entire document. Making mistakes or adding paragraphs are simple mouse clicks.

Good word processing software will allow you to do the following:

- Insert text
- Delete text
- Cut and paste text
- Copy
- Change page size and margins
- Search your document
- Automatic line return known as word wrap
- Print
- Change fonts
- Manage where files are located
- Make footnotes and references
- Insert graphics
- Create headers, footers, and page numbering
- Create different layouts
- Allow the merging of text from one file to another
- Use a spell checker
- Add table of contents and indexes
- Provide a thesaurus

There are many different word processing products available. The following will give you several to choose from, including free software programs.

MICROSOFT WORD

Word is the most popular Word Processor on the market. It has a large number of features and is easy to use. Since most people use this program, it is a good choice if you plan to share documents with others. Word 2007 will cost $149.99.

PLATE 1: MICROSOFT WORD

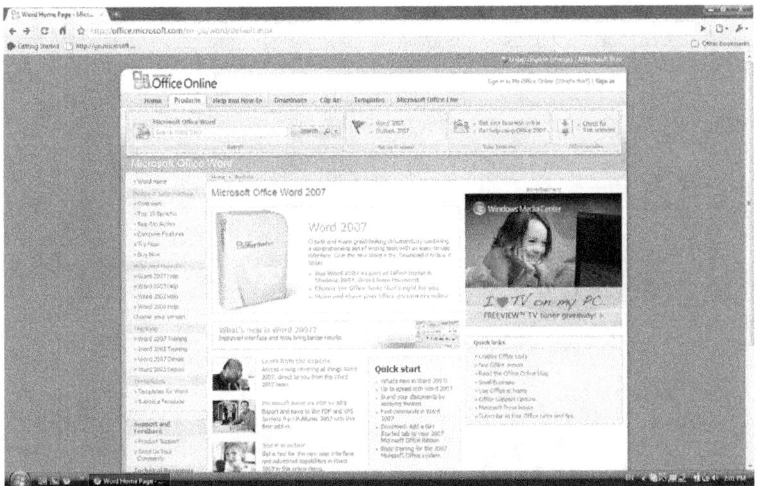

OPENOFFICE

OpenOffice.org 3.1 (www.openoffice.org) is a free office suite of software that includes word processing, spreadsheets, presentations, graphics, databases and more. It is easy to learn and compatible with other major word processing programs such as Word and WordPerfect. It can be downloaded for free and used for any purpose without restriction.

PLATE 2: OPENOFFICE

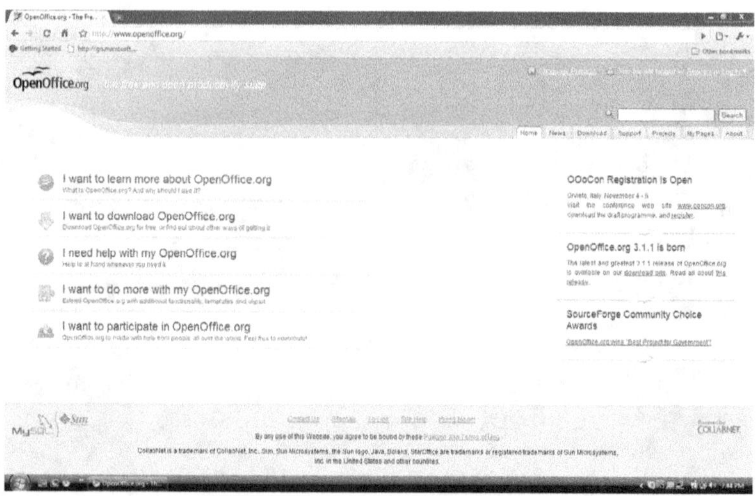

WORDPERFECT OFFICE X4

WordPerfect is software created by Corel and cannot be bought without purchasing the entire office suite. This program also has many different features and can be a good choice if you need a full office suite including spreadsheets, address books, dictionaries, and more since it is cheaper than Microsoft Word Office Suite.

Although Corel doesn't offer WordPerfect in a stand-alone version, the price of WordPerfect Office is extremely affordable for a full office suite. In addition to WordPerfect, the suite boasts a spreadsheet program, a presentation program, address book, and a dictionary. Word Perfect costs $269.99.

PLATE 3: WORD PERFECT

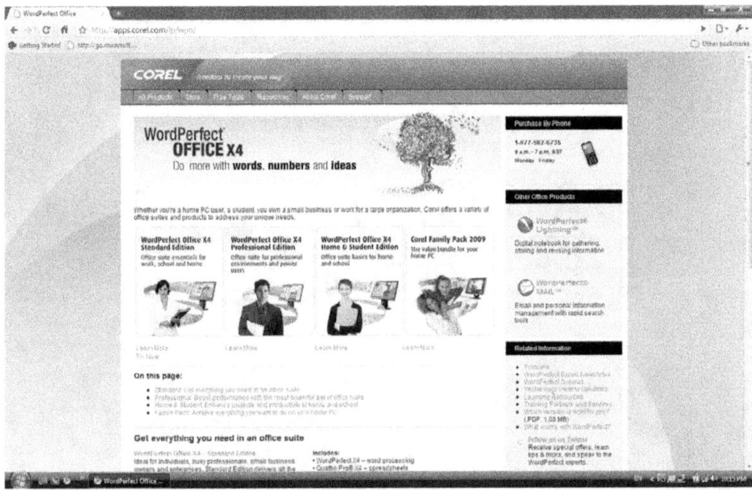

Web Browsers

Surfing the web is made possible by a *web browser*. Browsers are basically software programs that allow you to search for and view various kinds of information on the web, such as websites, video, audio, etc.

The most popular web browsers can be downloaded free of charge.

MICROSOFT'S INTERNET EXPLORER

Most Internet users are using Internet Explorer because it's easy to use and most websites are written with Internet Explorer in mind, meaning that they are compatible.

PLATE 4: MICROSOFT INTERNET EXPLORER

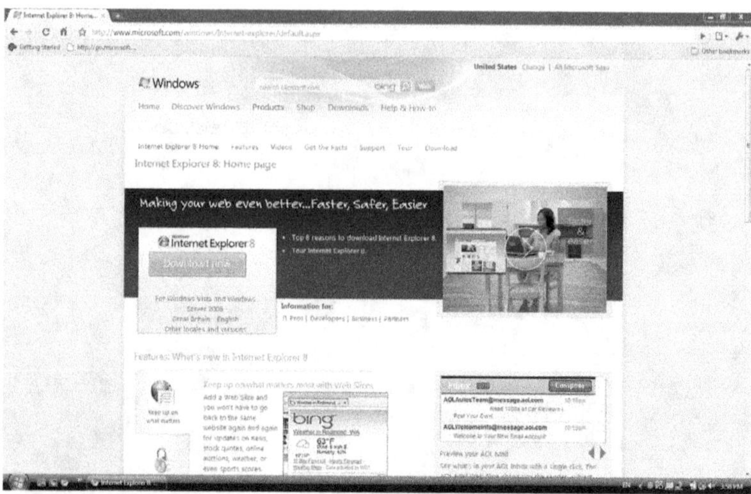

PLATE 5: MOZILLA FIREFOX

MOZILLA'S FIREFOX

Firefox is almost as popular as Internet Explorer and has tabbed browsing, superior security features, and fast loading.

MAC'S SAFARI

Specifically for Mac users, Safari is an excellent choice for a web browser, with fast load and good compatibility with most websites out there.

PLATE 6: MAC SAFARI

GOOGLE'S CHROME

Chrome is an Open Source browser which includes "isolated" tabs, designed to prevent browser crashes, and a more powerful JavaScript engine.

Plate 7: Google Chrome

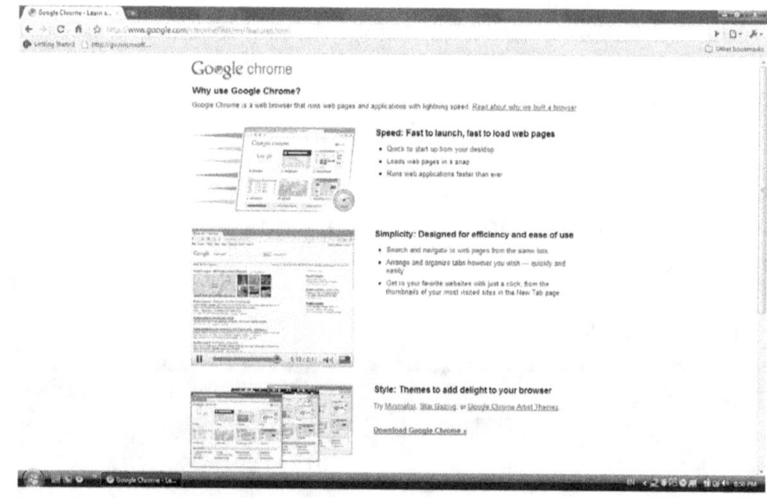

Email

Email stands for "electronic mail" and is often Internet-based; meaning that anyone with Internet access can receive and send email. It can also be in-house email that only reaches those within your organization. Email is a powerful, convenient and important communication tool.

Web-based email clients let you access your account from anywhere with just a browser. While you can read, write and reply to messages, the mail you receive is permanently kept at the online server so you can download and archive it back at your main computer. Here are some popular web-based email providers:

1. Gmail
2. Hotmail
3. Yahoo! Mail

PLATE 8: YAHOO! MAIL

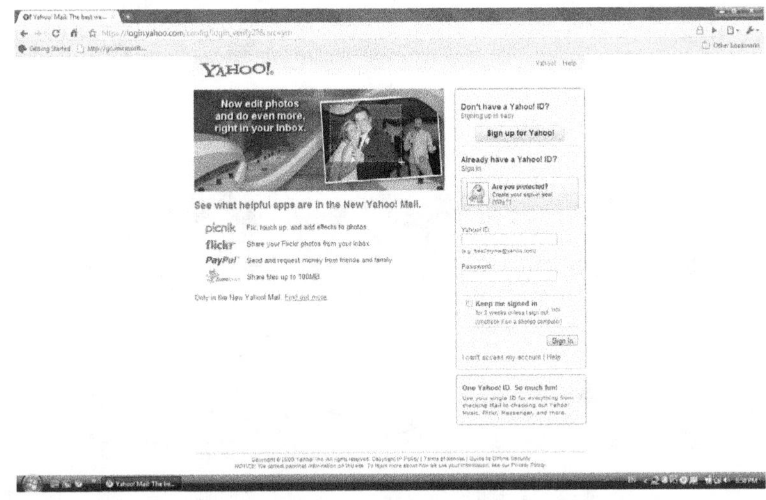

Another way to access email is through *desktop email*. Such programs only allow you to check your email from your own computer or with access to your own computer. Desktop email programs allow for more security and are an easier way to sort and store email in different files; for instance, having a file for 'Item Listed', 'Item Sold' or 'Payment Pending.'

The most popular desktop email programs include:

1. Outlook
2. Outlook Express
3. Mozilla Thunderbird
4. Eudora
5. Pegasus Mail

Microsoft Office Outlook is a great program though can be confusing to operate and it cannot create "smart folders" that learn what emails to put into what files, though this can be done manually by using its 'rules' function. The up and coming alternative is Mozilla Thunderbird, which has taken the good portions of Outlook and then created an easier interface as well as smart files.

PLATE 9: MOZILLA THUNDERBIRD

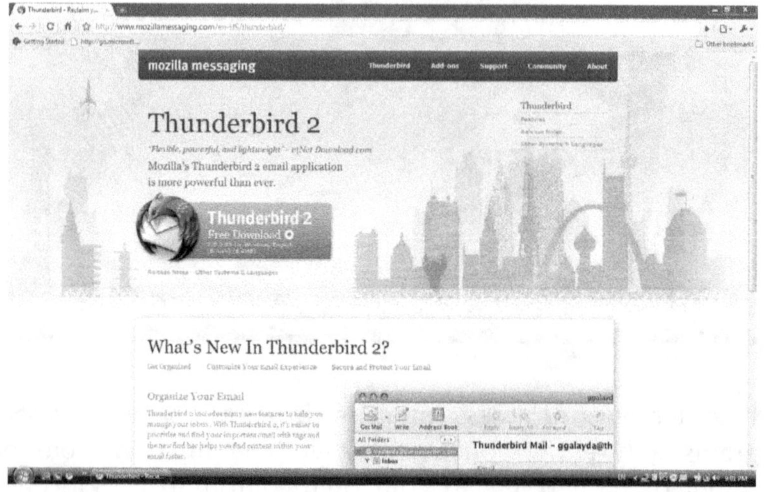

Image Editors

An *imaging editor* allows you to perform various image manipulation, editing or retouching features to refine, correct or enhance your existing image before including it in your website. You can perform various image editing operations such as:

- Flip, Crop or Rotate
- Apply Frames & Borders
- Change Brightness
- Contrast
- Resize
- Annotate (text on image)
- Change Image Format, etc.

Even if you haven't got a large budget, you can still enjoy a functional, well-designed image editor.

PLATE 10: ADOBE PHOTOSHOP

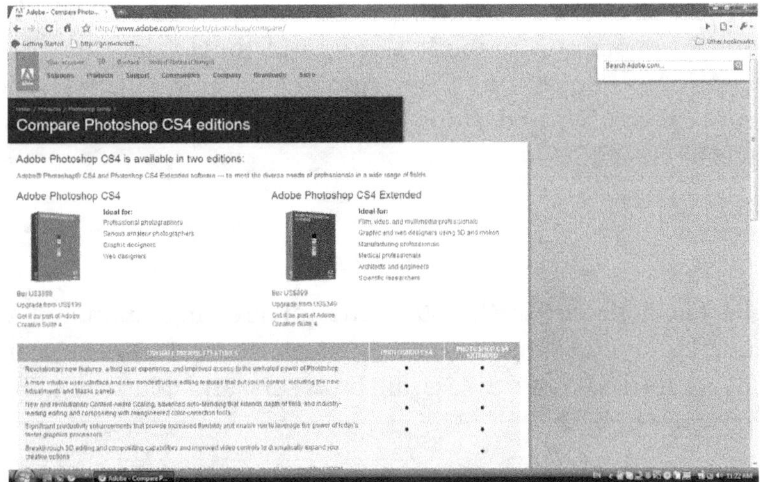

ADOBE PHOTOSHOP

Adobe Photoshop CS4 and Photoshop CS4 Extended meet the diverse needs of professionals in a wide range of fields. Photoshop offers unrivaled editing power with live filters, more precise color correction, easier black-and-white conversion, and more powerful cloning and healing tools. Photoshop will cost you between $319 to $999.

ADOBE PHOTOSHOP EXPRESS

Adobe Express is more cumbersome than some photo editors and takes a lot of time to switch between modes, upload photos, and preview changes. It does, however, allow photo uploads from Facebook, Photobucket and Picasa. This software program is a free download.

ADOBE FIREWORKS

Adobe Fireworks CS4 software creates and optimizes images for the web and rapidly prototyping websites and web applications. Fireworks CS4 offers the flexibility to edit both *vector* and *bitmap* images, has common prebuilt assets, and timesaving integration with Adobe Photoshop CS4, Adobe Illustrator CS4, Adobe Dreamweaver CS4, and Adobe Flash CS4 Professional software. Fireworks costs $299.

ADOBE FLASH

Adobe Flash Player is the standard for creating animated web content. Designs, animation, and application user interfaces can be deployed immediately across all browsers and platforms. Flash will cost $699.

COREL PHOTOPAINT

CorelDRAW Graphics Suite X4 is a photo editing application (including graphic design and page layout tools). At $429 the suite is expensive but is a favorite of many professional and amateur photographers alike.

SERIF PHOTOPLUS

Serif PhotoPlus 9 is a $9.99 photo editor with many high-end features. It also has help and simplified tools for beginners like quick fix, one-click red eye removal, auto-contrast, and extract tool. You can download earlier versions of PhotoPlus for free from freeserifsoftware.com to decide if you like it enough to purchase the latest version.

PLATE 11: WWW.FREESERIFSOFTWARE.COM

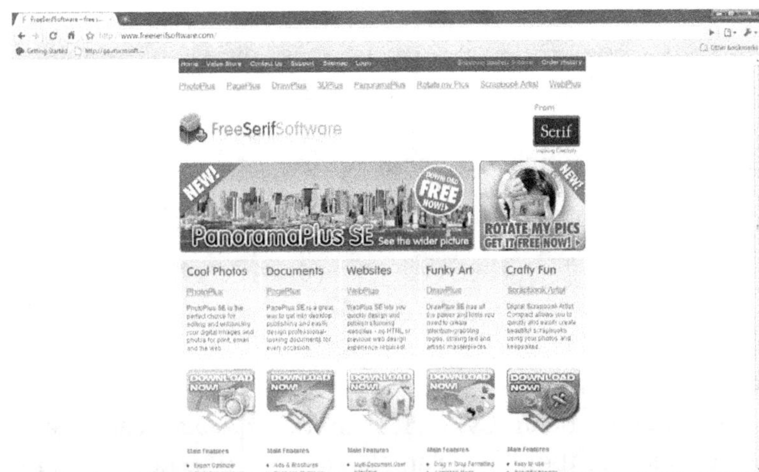

PAINT SHOP PRO

Corel Paint Shop Pro X is a good investment for digital photographers at any level. Although it is not as easy to use as some programs, you can purchase this software for $59.99. PaintShop Photo Express 2010 costs $49.99.

ULTIMATE PAINT

Ultimate Paint is very good for standard image creation, viewing, and manipulation. It features an image optimizer, image browser, over 100 image effects, and interactive print preview. From $34.95

GIMP FOR WINDOWS

GIMP is a popular open-source image editor originally developed for Unix/Linux. It is similar to Photoshop. Updates of this software could be an issue, but users have reported no significant problems.

PICASA

Picasa 3.5 is a powerful free software that helps you instantly find, edit and share all the pictures on your PC. Picasa will help you to keep track of your photos by sorting them into visual albums. You can also quickly touch up, email, print, or create CDs of your photos.

Spreadsheet Software

In order to know how much your company is spending in a certain area of the business, such as marketing, a spreadsheet is an excellent business tool. Data can also be stored to keep accounting simplified to make tax time easier.

A business can also use a spreadsheet for sales forecasting and financial analysis. Spreadsheets are not only used for numbers; they can help a business keep up with client and product lists, as well as due dates.

A *spreadsheet* organizes data into columns and rows, allowing users to easily display information and work with the data. For instance, you can sum up numbers or put lists into alphabetical order. Information can also be sorted and filtered. Businesses use spreadsheet programs to learn about different sets of information and to make decisions on a wide variety of topics.

MICROSOFT EXCEL

Microsoft Excel (overleaf) is the most widely used spreadsheet application. It is often bundled as part of the Microsoft Office suite of applications. It is excellent for calculations.

PLATE 12: MICROSOFT EXCEL SPREADSHEET

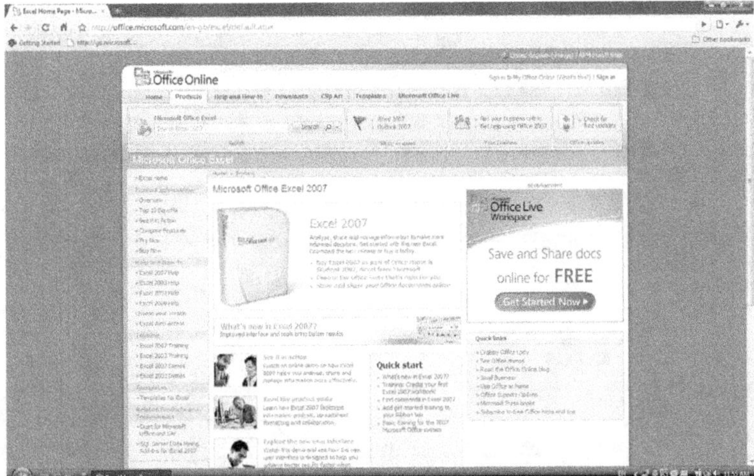

CALC

An *open source* and free alternative to Microsoft Excel is 'Calc', part of the OpenOffice applications suite. Open Source is a program with its source code available to the general public, for use and/or modification from its original design, free of charge.

Calc has many of the features of Microsoft's Excel, as well as provides some unique functions for graphs, based upon the input to the sheet.

Calc also has the capability to save the spreadsheet directly to Adobe PDF format, making the sheet more accessible and more easily shared across networks or the Internet.

Both Calc and Excel are multidimensional packages, meaning that different spreadsheets can be linked together using formulae. This can have the advantage of only having to update values in one spreadsheet that automatically updates other sheets.

PLATE 13: CALC SPREADSHEET

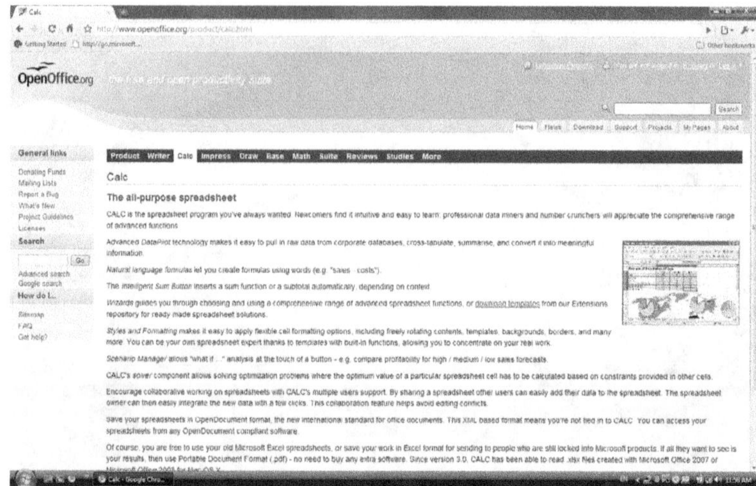

Anti-Virus Software

As stated earlier in the security section of this book, having antivirus protection for your computer is essential. Without such software, you will end up with malware that can destroy your system and cost your business significant time and money.

Antivirus software should be easy to use and install, should be able to seek out new virus threats, and clean infected files. There should also be help support available. Let's look at a few options.

THE SHIELD DELUXE

The Shield Deluxe 2009 v2 combines virus protection and spyware detection. The product is simple to install and set up, while offering advanced users a range of versatile settings for fine-tuning the program. The cost of Shield Deluxe is $39.99.

BITDEFENDER

BitDefender 2010 has a user-friendly interface that scans all existing files on your computer as well as all incoming and outgoing emails, IM transfers and all other network traffic. The cost of BitDefender is $29.95.

NORTON ANTI-VIRUS SOFTWARE 2010

Norton is easy to use and has wide-ranging security features to protect your PC from malicious programs including instant messaging scanning, script blocking and email protection. However, this software does not provide protection from network or file sharing transfers. Norton Antivirus costs $39.99.

PANDA

Panda Antivirus Pro 2010 is easy to use and has free automatic updates. It provides powerful blockage from hijackers, keyloggers, intruders, and hackers. Panda allows you to block, delete, clean, and quarantine infected files and does not slow your computer down during virus scans, allowing you to carry on working. The cost of Panda is $49.95.

MCAFEE

McAfee comes with a ScriptStopper, to stop viruses spreading from one computer to another via email, and WormStopper. Some downsides to the program are that it does not offer instant message (IM) protection, P2P/file sharing protection or registry start-up protection. McAfee does offer an 800 customer support number. The cost of McAfee is from $29.99.

AVAST

Avast Home Edition guards your computer and network with multiple shields that scan executables and files, IM, email, and more. You can select parameters for scanning, and even choose wildcards to exclude specific file types. It also has a simple user interface. The best part is that it is free.

KASPERSKY

Kaspersky Anti-Virus 2010 offers superior antivirus protection, has free and paid-for versions, and supports Windows 98 through Windows Vista. It is light and fast and consistently wins detection awards against the competition. The cost of Kaspersky is $39.95.

PLATE 14: KASPERSKY ANTI-VIRUS

Accounting Software

Accounting software has different modules dealing with different areas of accounting, such as:

- Accounts Receivable—where the company enters money received

- Accounts Payable—where the company enters its bills and pays money it owes

- General Ledger—the company's "books"

- Billing—where the company produces invoices to clients/customers

- Stock/Inventory—where the company keeps control of its inventory

- Purchase Order—where the company orders inventory

- Sales Order—where the company records customer orders for the supply of inventory

Additional modules offered by some software might include:

- Debt Collection—where the company tracks attempts to collect overdue bills

- Electronic Payment Processing

- Expense—where employee business-related expenses are entered

- Payroll—where the company tracks salary, wages, and related taxes

- Reports—where the company produces results, data and information

- Timesheet—where professionals record time worked so that it can be billed to clients

- Purchase Requisition—where requests for purchase orders are made, approved and tracked

At the low end of the business markets, inexpensive applications software allows most general business accounting functions to be performed. Some business accounting software is designed for specific business types. Though more expensive, it will include features that are specific to that industry.

Every small business needs to know where the money went - and is going. Let's look at a few top accounting programs to help you do just that.

PLATE 15: INTUIT QUICKBOOKS

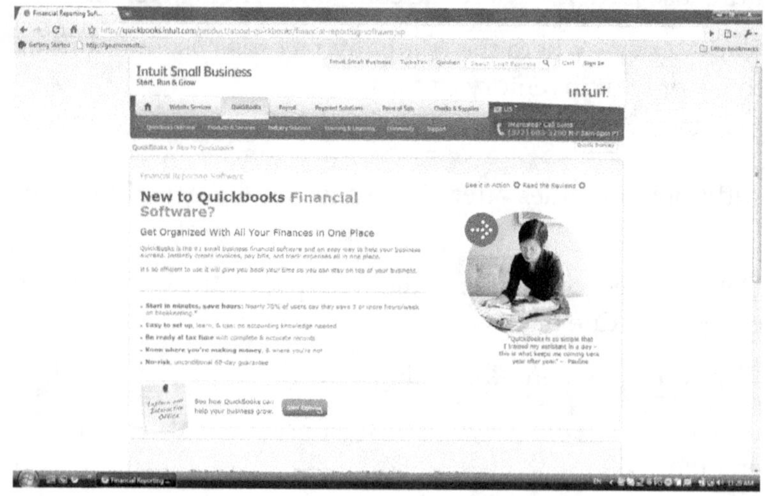

INTUIT QUICKBOOKS

QuickBooks by Intuit is a popular accounting and payroll program designed for small businesses. QuickBooks is available in Simple Start ($99.95), Online ($9.95 a month), Pro ($199.95), and Premier ($399.95) editions.

SIMPLY ACCOUNTING

Simply Accounting by Sage is an accounting and payroll package with all the features and reports any small business needs, including Internet and e-commerce features. This small business accounting software's data entry screens are similar to "paper" accounting and make it easy to learn. It can also be used by multiple users. Prices between $49.99 and $149.99.

PEACHTREE COMPLETE ACCOUNTING

The Complete version of this small business accounting software program includes over 125 reports and features such as in-depth inventory, time and billing and job costing. The accounting program comes multi-user ready and "value packs" for 5 or more users are available. Cost $219.99, although a Pro version with less features is available for $199.99.

MICROSOFT OFFICE ACCOUNTING

Microsoft Office Accounting 2009 integrates with other Microsoft software. So, if you are currently using Excel or Outlook, Accounting 2009 will be able to use data already entered into these and other Microsoft Office products. Cost $199.95.

Note: There is also a QuickBooks Simple Start FREE version:

QUICKBOOKS SIMPLE START

QuickBooks accounting software for small business allows you to keep track of sales, receipts and expenses. The package allows you to raise quotes and invoices, keep up to date tax-related income and expenses, and print reports. The software is user friendly. To select the function you want, just click on the icons representing each activity on a dashboard. You also get technical support for the first 30 days.

Web Editing Software

If you are planning to create a website, you should invest in a good web editing program. Since web technology is rapidly changing, always look for and purchase the most recent versions of the software. If you are using earlier versions, you should definitely think about upgrading.

EXPRESSIONS WEB BY MICROSOFT

Expression Web 3 is the newest web editing software from Microsoft. It comes highly recommended and is designed with serious as well as new web developers in mind. Express Web 3 costs $149.

FRONTPAGE 2003 BY MICROSOFT

This is a tried and trusted option but, as an alternative, the most recent release of web editing software from Microsoft is Expressions Web. This software is easy to use and the price is less than $200.

PLATE 16: DREAMWEAVER CS4

DREAMWEAVER CS4 BY ADOBE

Dreamweaver is the industry standard for web professionals. Developers can use Dreamweaver with the server technology of their choice to build powerful Internet applications that connect users to databases, web services etc. Dreamweaver costs $250-399.

GOLIVE BY ADOBE

GoLive is an older product from Adobe and has now largely been replaced with Dreamweaver. However, this program has a very good Mac version. You can work with Adobe Photoshop, Adobe Illustrator, and Adobe Portable Document Format (PDF) files directly within GoLive, without switching between applications. This software is currently difficult to buy except through websites such as eBay.

NVU

Nvu (pronounced N-view, for a "new view") makes managing a website easy for those without technical experience or knowledge of *HTML* (the programming language used to create documents for display on the Internet). It is a complete web authoring system for Linux Desktop users as well as Microsoft Windows and Macintosh users. Nvu is FREE.

KOMPOZER

KompoZer is designed to be extremely easy to use, making it ideal for non-technical computer users who want to create an attractive, professional-looking website without needing to know HTML or web coding. KompoZer is FREE.

FTP Software

FTP (File Transfer Protocol) is the simplest and most secure way to exchange files over the Internet. Whether you know it or not, you most likely use FTP all the time. The ability to transfer files back-and-forth makes FTP essential for anyone creating a web page as this is the software that will upload your web pages to your website.

When downloading a file from the Internet you're actually transferring the file to your computer from another computer over the Internet. This is why the T (transfer) is in FTP. To make an FTP connection you can use a standard web browser (Internet Explorer, Firefox, etc.) or a dedicated FTP software program, referred to as an FTP *client*.

An FTP Client is software that is designed to transfer files back-and-forth between two computers over the Internet. It needs to be installed on your computer and can only be used with a live connection to the Internet.

PLATE 17: CLASSIC FTP TWO-PANE DESIGN

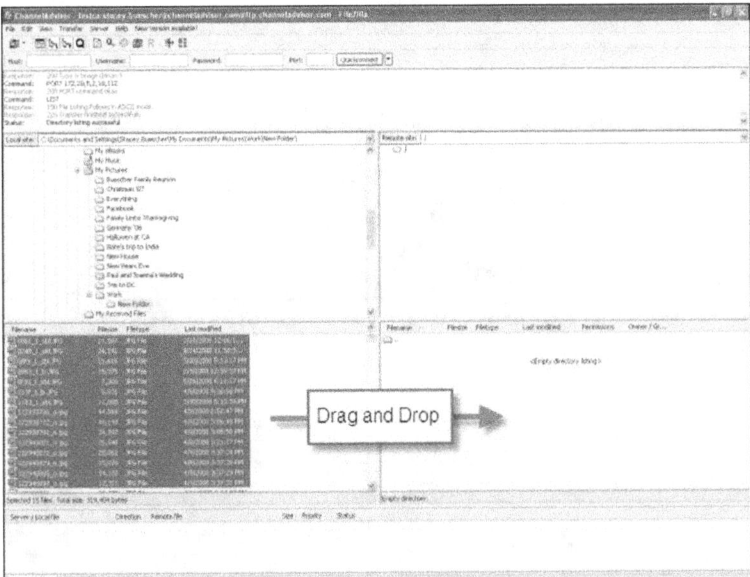

The classic FTP Client look is a two-pane design. The pane on the left displays the files on your computer and the pane on the right displays the files on the remote computer.

File transfers are as easy as dragging-and-dropping files from one pane to the other or by highlighting a file and clicking one of the direction arrows located between the panes.

Here are just a few of the FTP clients you may choose from:

WS_FTP

WS_FTP Professional is the choice for high-end needs. WS_FTP Professional supports 128-bit SSL encryption, simple installation wizards and a full administrative *GUI*. It also features a built-in log analyzer. WS_FTP is designed to run on true Windows servers; it runs on Windows NT, 2000, XP and Vista. WS_FTP Professional costs $89.95.

PLATE 18: WS_FTP

WAR FTP DAEMON

War FTP Daemon is free FTP software. It runs on most popular versions of Windows and is designed for a range of needs from basic to advanced. War FTP has been developed over many years and has proven itself as a stable and mature *freeware* Windows FTP server.

ZFTPSERVER SUITE

zFTPServer Suite is a free Windows FTP server. It features multi-lingual user interfaces, flexible access control for both accounts and IP addresses, and passive as well as active mode connections. zFTPServer supports all popular Windows operating systems (including Vista) and is designed for ease of use by beginning and intermediate level users.

FILEZILLA SERVER

Windows FTP server download, FileZilla Server is a free, Open Source program. It offers both binary and full source code downloads. FileZilla Server tracks the user IDs of all connected sessions and each file transferred.

SERV-U FTP SERVER

Serv-U strikes a good balance between cost, features, and stability. Serv-U runs on all popular versions of Windows including Windows 95 and Windows 98 as well as Windows NT and the newer Windows platforms. Costs $199.95.

DREAMWEAVER CS4

The website development software Dreamweaver also has a built-in FTP facility which is extremely easy to use. It will cost between $212 and $375.49 or you can buy it as part of the Adobe Creative Suite 4, which includes all the development applications you will ever need for between $999 and $1,579.99.

PDF Software

Many companies plan to sell *e-books*. An e-book is a book published in electronic form, similar to a Word document, which can be delivered to any computer that is connected to the Internet from anywhere in the world. However, to keep an e-book secure so that it maintains its formatting and stops others from copying the book, a PDF format is often used.

PDF stands for Portable Document Format. PDFs have a number of advantages over other file formats. They are designed for on-screen reading, print well and are virus resistant. PDF documents are created using PDF software; therefore, if your company will be selling e-books or creating other online documents, you will need PDF software.

PLATE 19: ADOBE ACROBAT

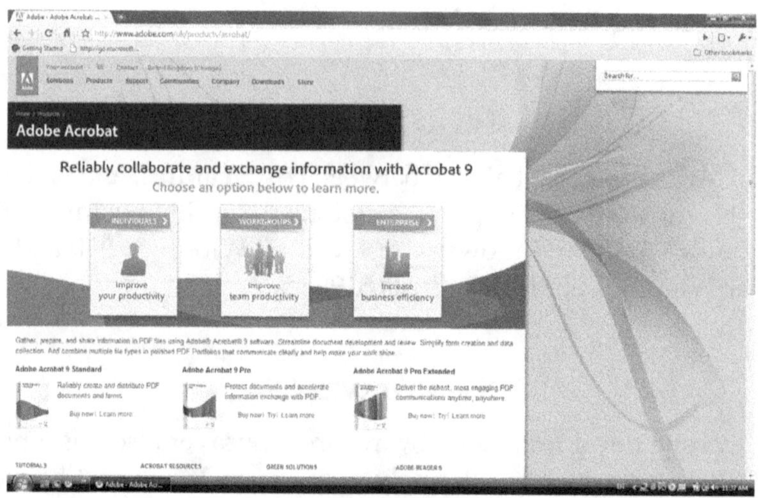

ADOBE ACROBAT

Adobe Acrobat is a program or suite of programs from Adobe Systems, Inc. which creates, edits, and manipulates PDF files. Users looking for full-featured PDF creation software will want to consider Adobe Acrobat 9, a product that has become synonymous with the PDF format. Users can add password protection to documents and specify an expiration date for documents, as well as assign myriad other security policies. Adobe Acrobat 9 Pro costs $449.

PDF 995

The Pdf995 suite of products - Pdf995, PdfEdit995, and Signature995 - is a complete solution for document publishing. It provides ease of use, flexibility in format, and industry-standard security. Pdf995 makes it easy and affordable to create professional-quality documents in the popular PDF file format. Its easy-to-use interface helps you to create PDF files by simply selecting the "print" command from any application, creating documents, which can be viewed on any computer with a PDF viewer. Pdf995 is FREE.

PRIMO PDF

PrimoPDF 4 converts just about any file type to a PDF, using the source program the file was created with and its print command. The interface is easy to navigate and users can choose to email the PDF instantly after its creation. The conversion process from whatever document is on your screen to PDF is quick and efficient. PrimoPDF is FREE.

Shopping Carts

A web-based *shopping cart* is a way for customers to read a list of products and mark off the selections they want. Then, when they are finished, they can check out and review their tax, shipping, and total order.

Shopping cart software is the programming that allows a website to build a catalog of products and its database and integrate it into its website pages. The shopping cart is one of the most important parts to having a smooth e-commerce transition since it is how your customers will ultimately purchase your products.

If you are looking for a shopping cart solution for your website, there are many choices available. Many hosting companies provide shopping cart applications as a part of their e-commerce hosting packages. If not, or if the shopping cart does not suit your needs, you will have to either purchase shopping cart software or find a hosted solution.

Before you start shopping for a cart solution, make a list of what you need your cart to do:

- Can you install and configure the cart software yourself, or will you need help?

- How many transactions do you think you will have? Some software handles a larger volume than others.

- Will it work with your current online store?

- How much can you afford to pay for a shopping cart?

- What level of security and encryption will you, and your customers, be comfortable with?

These are only a handful of the questions that may arise when you look for a shopping cart solution, but they will help guide you in selecting the right cart application for your needs.

The first question is probably the most significant. If you are tech-savvy and feel comfortable setting up your own shopping cart, you will be able to take advantage of one of the many free, open-source carts out there. But if you need a hosted solution, that will take you in another direction entirely.

Below are some open source Carts:

OSCOMMERCE

osCommerce is the leading Open Source online shop e-commerce solution that is available for free under the GNU General Public License. It features a rich set of out-of-the-box online shopping cart functionality that allows store owners to set up, run, and maintain online stores with minimum effort and with no costs, fees, or limitations involved. osCommerce is FREE.

ZenCart

The developers of ZenCart set out to make it easier to install and use for non-tech-types. ZenCart lets you spotlight specific items in your store, making it very useful for product promotions. The three-step checkout process is easy to understand and use. ZenCart is FREE.

PLATE 20: ZENCART

PhpShop

This program is full of features and is easy to install and maintain. PhpShop is FREE.

Below are some third-party solutions:

PayPal

Offers shopping cart capability as part of their package. The cart is free, but it requires that your buyers pay via PayPal which means you will owe PayPal a transaction fee. However, the fees are reasonable, and the cart is fairly easy to set up and use.

MONSTERCOMMERCE

MonsterCommerce is a complete shopping cart solution. In addition to a full-featured shopping cart, you can also have MonsterCommerce host your website. MonsterCommerce has a $99 activation fee.

PLATE 21: X-CART

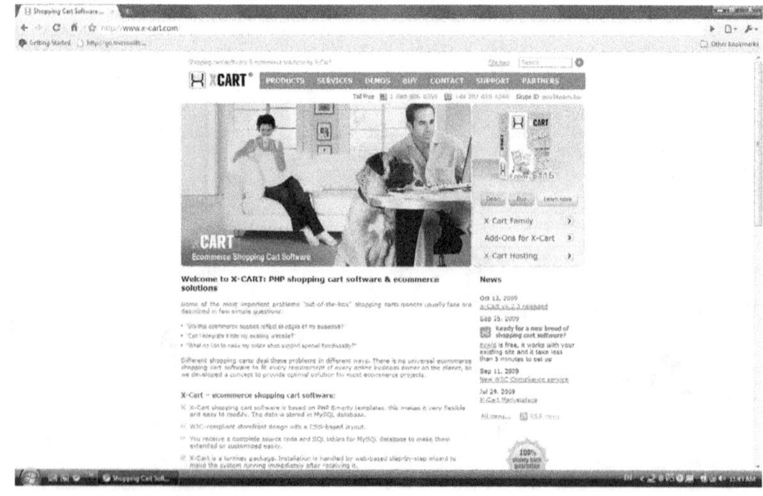

X-CART

X-Cart is a well-established shopping cart package with a comprehensive range of features (gift certificates, special offers etc.). It comes with its php/CSS code fully editable, so it can be customized however you wish. It's multilingual and comes in a variety of 'skins' (i.e. shopfront designs and themes), with an unlimited catalog size. It also has several add-ons, such as an integrated affiliate scheme. X-Cart costs $229.

Here are some total shopping cart solutions:

MICROSOFT COMMERCE MANAGER

Microsoft Commerce Manager has many features to create an online storefront. You can also list products on the auction block and on shopping sites, as well as list them on your website. You can also provide customers with an order status. It costs $249 per year or $24.95 per month.

YAHOO! MERCHANT SOLUTIONS

Merchant Solutions offers single or multi-page checkout, automatic calculations for shipping and tax, support for downloadable products, custom design options, and even gift-wrapping options. Yahoo! Merchant Solutions costs $39.95 per month with a 1.5% transaction fee and a $50 set-up fee.

PLATE 22: YAHOO! MERCHANT SOLUTIONS

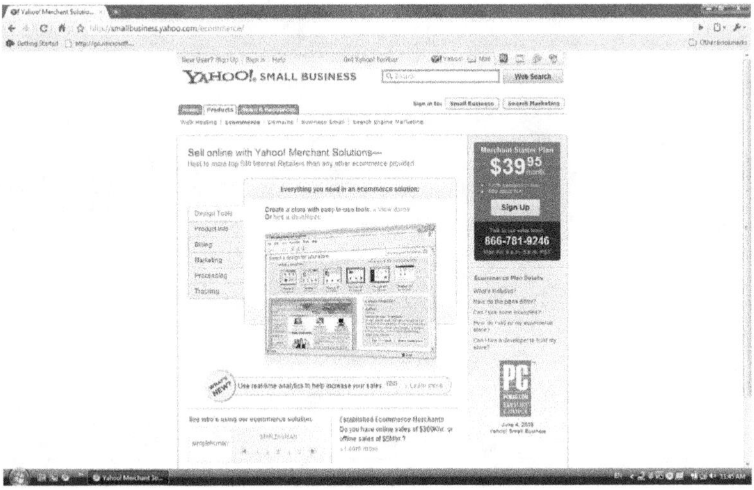

"Risk comes from not knowing what you're doing."
Warren Buffet

5

Hosting

Once you have your equipment, software, and Internet connection, you will need to determine how you will host your website. A simple definition of *web hosting* is a service that provides, at a minimum, storage space on a *server* (specialized computer) and bandwidth, which allows the data (web pages, images, etc) stored on this server to be transferred to anyone viewing the data. In other words, it provides your website with an Internet connection so that it can be accessed by anyone with an Internet connection.

What to Consider

Web hosts exist to provide a bundle of services that make publishing on the Internet possible. Web hosts combine many services logically into a single package at a reasonable price.

These services typically include:

- **Storage space -** The physical disk space on a server where your website data (pages, images, scripts, emails etc) is stored

- **Bandwidth** - The Internet traffic and the networking infrastructure needed to deliver the traffic to users of your website

- **Email accounts** - Email boxes where you can send and receive email. Often many other email service variations are provided as well

- **Technical support** - A staff of support technicians to help you with general service usage issues and other problems as they arise

- **Scripting support** - The ability to run scripts (small programs that perform certain tasks) on the server

- **Backup services** - A service that makes a copy of your website data in case of accidental deletion or other emergency situation

Web hosting is often provided as part of a general Internet access plan; there are many free and paid for providers offering these services. Bought services are more reliable and better for most small businesses and cost $10 or less per month, depending on what you use it for. Large, complex websites with resource-sapping applications or databases may cost more to have hosted.

Renting a server from an Internet Service Provider (ISP) is a common option. Below are some advantages:

- Very fast connections to the Internet

- Powerful web servers

- Minimum 99% up time

- Latest software patches

- Best virus protection

When choosing a hosting company, you will want to have the following:

- 24-hour support with toll-free phone service

- Daily backup

- No fees for high traffic volume on your website

- Enough bandwidth to allow image files, video and sound

- Email capabilities

- Access to your database software

Web Hosting Companies

PLATE 23: WWW.HOSTGATOR.COM

Affordable website hosting is readily available across the net. The top ten best web hosting companies in the USA for 2009 were:

Rank	Top Web Hosts	Features
1	**HostGator.com**	¤ 600 GB of space ¤ 6000 GB traffic ¤ $9.95 / month
2	**BlueHost.com**	¤ 1500 GB space ¤ 15000 GB traffic ¤ $6.95 / month
3	**LunarPages.com**	¤ 1500 GB starage ¤ 15000 GB traffic ¤ $6.95 / month
4	**WebHostingBuzz**	¤ 375 GB space ¤ 5000 GB traffic ¤ $3.95 / month
5	**Dot5Hosting.com**	¤ 1500 GB storage ¤ 15000 GB traffic ¤ $4.95 / month
6	**EasyCGI.com**	¤ 350 GB of space ¤ 3500 GB traffic ¤ $7.96 / month
7	**1and1.com**	¤ 10 GB web space ¤ 300 GB of traffic ¤ $3.99 / month
8	**iPower.com**	¤ 1500 GB storage ¤ 15000 GB traffic ¤ $7.95 / month
9	**PowWeb.com**	¤ 1500 GB space ¤ 15000 GB traffic ¤ $5.77 / month
10	**ResellersPanel.com**	¤ 15 GB disk space ¤ 300 GB of traffic ¤ $3.33 / month

6

Creating an Online Presence

If you are serious about making your business as successful as it can be then you need to have a web presence. Being online will help project a professional image and expand your potential market place well beyond your local area.

Registering a domain name will also help protect your business name or brand name and branded goods or services. Once you have decided on your online strategy you will then need to do the following:

- **Register a domain name**: Visit InterNIC (www.internic.net/regist.html) to find a registrar of domain names where you can register your chosen website address. The InterNIC website is run by ICANN, the Domain Name System (DNS) registration service. Try to register a .com domain, as the '.com' suffix still carries the most prestigious and well-recognized of all the suffixes for a business website. Unfortunately, many domain names with the suffix .com are not available, but if your name is original enough you may be able to get just what you want. Otherwise, be prepared to try multiple variations. Here's a tip: if your name is not available, for example www.domaincosts.com, try using dashes; www.domain-costs.com or www.costs-domain.com. Typically, a .com domain name will cost you about $20 for 2 years.

- **Host your website**: As stated in the previous section, this can cost from $40 to $120 per year.

PLATE 24: WWW.INTERNIC.NET/REGIST.HTML

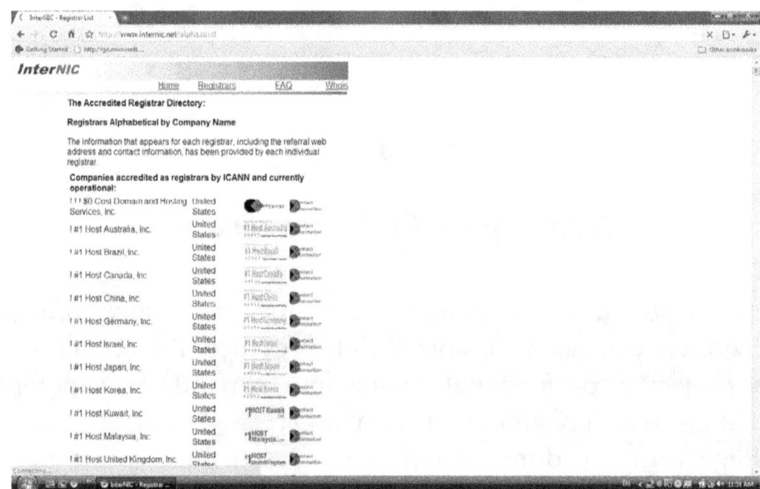

Website Development

Next, you should consider the cost of developing the website; this can be accomplished in one of two ways. One option is to hire a web design company or developer to create and manage your website. These fees will vary depending on the size and skills of the company or developer you hire.

Expect to pay at least $750 for a simple 5 page website if you use a local company. As a way to estimate, figure on a $100 per page. This is an average price. Some companies end up paying more, depending on the complexity of their website.

For example, a website designed to display photographs and text is relatively simple to create, while a website that includes archiving capabilities, live databases, e-commerce capabilities and other interactive tools can be quite time-consuming to create and will cost more money.

Outsourcing your development work offshore is becoming much more of a reasonable and practical option. Using outsourcing services, such as Elance (www.elance.com), can considerably reduce your development and maintenance costs.

The other option involves creating a website on your own, using design software programs. With such software, it takes only basic computer literacy skills to create a website from scratch. It is really a matter of learning the program you have chosen.

You may also choose to use a template website, typically found in some hosting packages. With such a website, you can choose your website design from a collection of website templates.

PLATE 25: WWW.ELANCE.COM

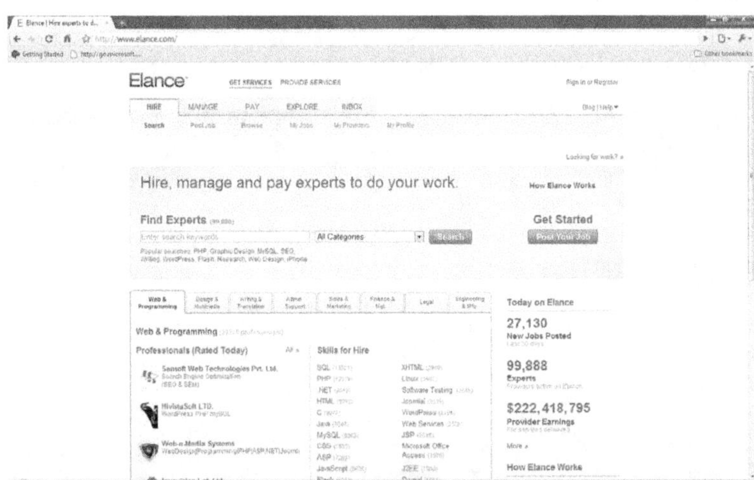

There are a few initial start-up costs associated with creating a new website, but in most cases, the entire website will cost less than $175 to create and maintain for the first year. After the website is developed, yearly maintenance costs average less than $75 per year, although that will depend on the amount of content updating etc. required.

Another benefit from opting to create a website on your own, apart from the lower cost, is the ability to create the website exactly the way you want it to be. When working with a designer, your vision can get lost or misinterpreted.

Website Content

One aspect of website design that many people fail to consider is the website's content. If you are a writer you may be able to provide your own content. If you do not have the time, desire, or literary skills, you will probably want to hire a professional content provider.

PLATE 26: WWW.FREELANCE.COM

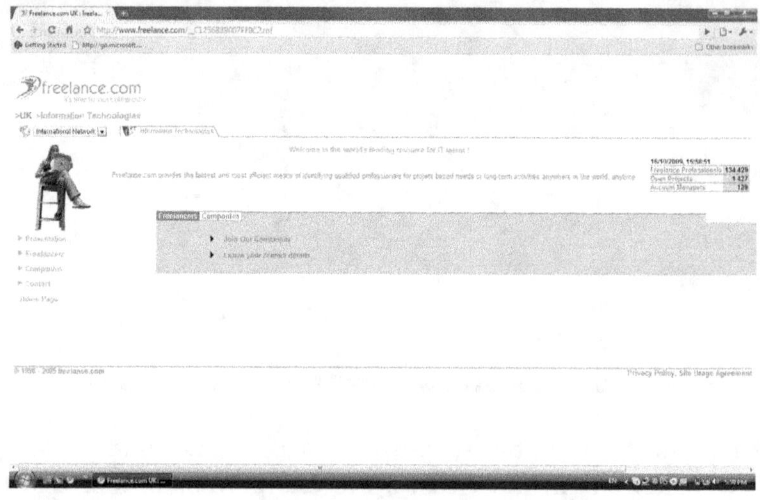

If you have a wonderfully designed website but it has poor grammar and spelling, or incomplete sentences, your website will not portray the professionalism you seek.

Freelance writer and editor rates range from a low of $25 an hour up to $250 an hour, or more. You should definitely shop around. One good place to find freelance writers for a reasonable amount of money is www.freelance.com.

Providing imagery for your website is another area where, rather than take the photos or create the images yourself, you might want to consider using stock photographs and images. There are several stock image companies on the net; for example, iStockphoto (www.istockphoto.com) is an excellent resource for copyright-free images.

PLATE 27: WWW.ISTOCKPHOTO.COM

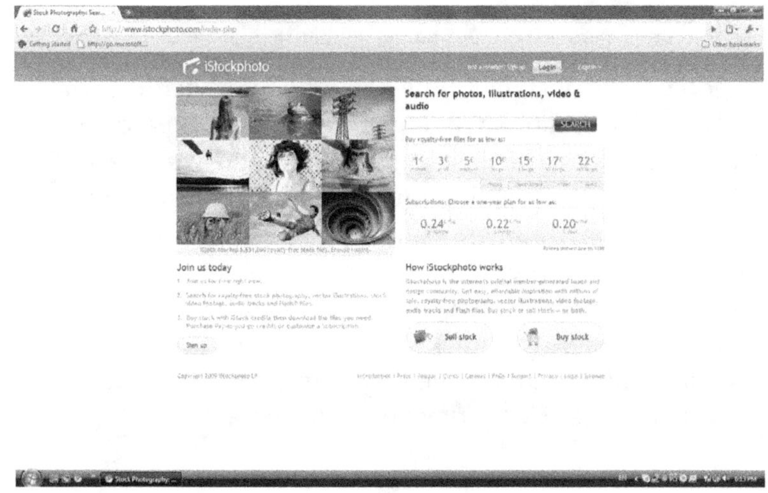

Website Maintenance

Finally, many businesses do not consider the cost of maintaining a website. The cost of maintaining your website over a 12-month period needs to be added to your budget so that your website, and ultimately your business, has the chance to achieve its goals.

For some businesses the maintenance costs are not high, for others they can far exceed the development cost. The cost of maintaining a website will vary due to many factors. They could include:

- The size and complexity of your website

- How often you make changes

- The need to add new products or pages

- How often you want the website's content or inventory indexed

- Your online marketing costs

A good web designer will provide rates before doing any work. These rates may vary depending on the type of work you need to have done. The cost of maintaining a website is so very individual that it is difficult to quote a price. Website firms charge by the hour for updates and there is typically a one-hour minimum charge involved.

Maintaining a website *in-house* allows your business to update the website frequently, quickly, and cheaply. There are several commercial content management systems (CMSs) available or you can have a bespoke system developed for you.

The Dos & Don'ts for Website Success

Do:

- Invest in a secure online ordering system.
- Keep your audience in mind and create copy that speaks to them personally.
- Update your website content and keep it fresh and current.
- Check your website to ensure all forms and links are working.
- Include your contact information.
- Offer a link to programs such as Acrobat Reader if it is required to view your website's content.
- Choose a web host that provides exceptional service, minimal down time, and consistent website backups.
- Carefully check your content for spelling and grammatical mistakes.

Don't:

- Confuse your visitor with too many topics or offers on one page.
- Let your website become outdated.
- Include too many colors, fonts, or font sizes that distract your visitors.
- Yell at your visitor by using all capital letters.
- Ignore or delay customer requests.
- Include graphics that fail to improve your website.
- Add unnecessary "extras" that will take a particularly long time to load.

Note: For a more comprehensive list of the 'Dos & Don'ts' of website success, visit www.riskeliminator.com

Costs

Although costs of the different components have been stated throughout this section, here is a representation of your initial and ongoing costs to start your online business over the first 12-month period:

Item	Cost
Computer	$500 to $1200
Printer	Free (+ PC package) $400
Scanner	$35 to $200
Digital Camera	$40 to $350
Internet Connection	$120 to $360
Word Processing	Free to $150
Image Editor	Free to $79
Spreadsheet	Free to $155
Anti-Virus	Free to $80
Accounting	Free to $300
Web Editing	Free to $399
PDF	Free to $299
Shopping Carts	Free to $500
FTP	Free to $100
Hosting	$40 to $120
Website Creation	$175 to $3000 or more
Website Content	Free to $500
Website Content	Free to $500
Website Maintenance	$75 to $2000 or more
Total Setup & Equipment Costs	**$985 to $10,342 or more***

* Prices are correct at the time of publishing.

As you can see, there is a big difference between the least expensive way to get started and buying the "best" of everything. The cheapest way is not always the best way; however, knowing what choices you have and what options are available to you will help you determine the best *Strategic Fit*™ for your business.

Thankfully, many times, the best fit happens to be the free, open-source software option. Therefore, try to budget accurately before overspending on equipment and software you may not need.

Summary

Although you may look at the initial costs and wonder if being online is truly necessary, the answer is that it most definitely is. Being online means:

1. Your business is open to everyone all the time. No matter what time of day or night, no matter what the day of the week, no matter where your customers live, you have the opportunity to meet their needs.

2. No matter what you sell, it can be updated immediately, anytime and there is no need to reprint expensive promotional materials.

3. You can easily reach out to new markets. On the Internet, you aren't just a local little business anymore.

4. Your customer service will improve because you can answer questions on your website rather than a customer having to contact you.

5. Your website provides you with a professional image. This will instill confidence in your clients that you are able to do for them what needs to be done.

6. Selling in cyberspace is cheaper than selling in a "brick-n-mortar" business with rent, electric bills, and other costs. And even if you have a "brick-n-mortar" business, you can supplement your business with an extra volume of sales.

7. If you have a service-oriented business, you can promote your business online. Millions of users are referring to the web and are using companies' websites to make major decisions when they need a specialized service.

8. You can gather information about your customers using forms and surveys so that you can offer targeted products or services based on customer feedback.

9. If you offer downloadable products, you can fulfill the modern need of instant gratification. You can even offer free samples or trials to download.

10. Finally, e-commerce is the future; online retail sales are predicted to rise to over $300 billion by 2010. You'd be missing an incredible, once-in-a-lifetime, opportunity if you don't create an e-commerce business or giving your established business an e-commerce capability.

Checklist

1. Computer with appropriate hard drive, RAM, and platform
2. Printer
3. Scanner
4. Digital Camera
5. Modem or Ethernet Card
6. Internet Connection
7. Word Processing Software
8. Web Browser
9. Email
10. Image Editor Software
11. Spreadsheet Software
12. Anti-Virus Software
13. Accounting Software
14. Web Editing Software
15. FTP Software
16. PDF Software
17. Shopping Cart Software
18. Disaster Recovery Plan
19. Copyright, Trademark or Patent your Intellectual Property
20. Hosting
21. Web Development
22. Web Content and Content Management System
23. Web Maintenance, strategy and budget

Note: If you intend selling products and services directly from your website, then you may want to:

1. Form a company
2. Acquire a business bank account
3. Set up a credit card processing facility

The costs for these are detailed in Part Two of this book, 'How to Form a Company'.

"Risk comes from not knowing what you're doing."
Warren Buffet

Part Two

How to Form a Company

The initial step towards establishing an online business is to form a company. This section will teach you just that.

Firstly, concentrate on developing your business idea, because until you know exactly what you are selling, and how you're going to sell it, you shouldn't decide on a name.

You also need to decide whether promoting your brand name is going to help you sell more units than if you were to promote what you are offering. For example, a consumer will often buy a well-known brand because they trust it. However, that same consumer will buy the same product from a different retailer if they consider the alternative offer too good to turn down.

The question to ask is, 'Is my offer stronger than my brand?' If it is, or you do not have an established brand, then it may be more advantageous to name your business, and more importantly your website, after the product, service or offer you intend promoting.

Consider, are you more likely to buy a widget from widget.com or jonesandwilliamsstores.com if you've never heard of Jones & Williams Stores? It's more likely that you'll assume that since widget.com just sell widgets, then they are more likely to sell good widgets at a good price. Consumers also tend to assume that websites that specialize in one specific product or service will offer a more expert and thorough product knowledge, customer service and after-sales support for that product or service.

7

Choosing a Name

If you don't already have an established brand name that you are commercially committed to, one of the most exciting decisions you will make before opening your website's doors is naming your business. The name of your business is the vital "first impression" a prospective client will have of you. Therefore, choose a name that reflects what you do or what you sell.

Here are four tips for determining a good name for your online business:

1. Is it memorable? A business name is one of the first things that a person learns when they learn of your business. When they walk away, you want them to remember the name and desire the service.

2. Can nine out of 10 people spell it? This is important. If they cannot spell your business name, then they will not be able to find you on the Internet. How can you determine if you have a spellable name? Take a survey. Tell people your name and ask them to spell it. If nine people can spell it for every 10 people you ask, then you have a winner. If not, you need to rethink your name.

3. What image does it create for others? Ask people this question, "When I say the name, what do you think of?" If they have the right idea, it is a good name. Rethink the name if

they come up with something totally different. You might think your name is cute and catchy, but it may confuse others. If your business name does not convey your product or service, you may miss out on prospective clients.

4. Does it represent all that you do now and all that you plan to do in the future? When you name your business you want the name to mean something to the person who hears it, without creating a name that is too limiting. For example, you may not want to be ABC Widgets if you think that you will soon be selling something more than widgets.

Choosing Your Domain Name

The last tip when choosing your company name is to get a good *domain name*. Before you rush out and choose your domain name you need to consider many different factors.

Your Domain Name is Your Online Brand Name

Naming your site after your domain may seem obvious to some of you, but you'll be surprised to learn that not every website is named after the domain name. Naming a site after its domain name is important, for the simple reason that when people think of your website, they'll think of it by name.

Imagine that your business is called "Widgets", but somebody else holds that domain name. Instead, you have some obscure domain name called, say, "gooditemsforsale.com". What happens when your customers, recalling that Widgets has a product they want, type "www.widgets.com"? They'll wind up at your competitor's website. One lost sale.

In the modern world of the Internet, where people automatically turn to the web for information, it pays to have a domain name that reflects your site or business. There are just fewer things for your customers or visitors to remember.

What if you cannot get the domain name of your choice? It really depends on how committed you are to that particular name. If you have an existing brand name that you're known for, you'll probably not want to ditch that name just because you can't get the domain name. After all, it may have taken you a lot of time and money to establish that name.

If so, you might simply want to try to buy the domain name from the current owner. Check up the "whois" information for the domain, and contact that person listed to see if they're willing to sell it. You probably should be aware that they are likely to want to charge a higher fee than you'll normally get when buying new domains (assuming they want to sell it in the first place).

PLATE 28: WWW.WHOIS.NET

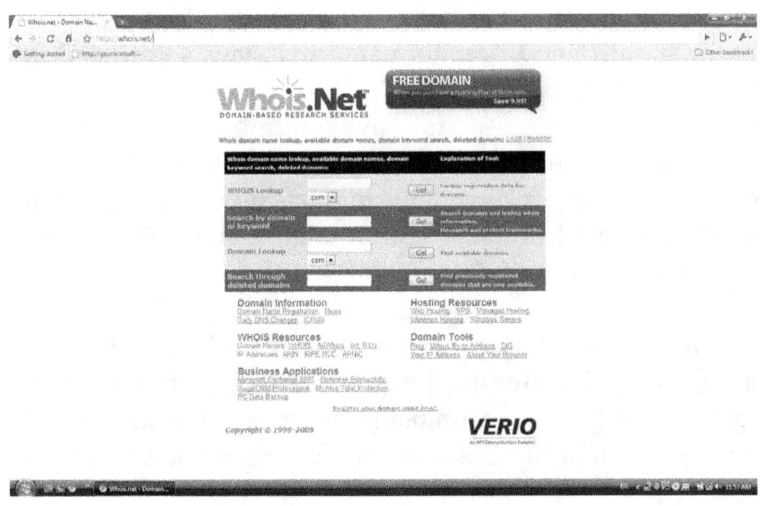

On the other hand, if you're just starting out, you might prefer the cheaper alternative of trying to obtain a domain name first, and then naming your website (or business) after the domain that you've acquired. So if you've acquired, say, the domain name "widgets.com", then your website and business might be named "Widgets" or "widgets.com".

I know this seems a bit like putting the cart before the horse, but that's the reality if you don't want to lose out on the Internet; what you sell, and the offer you make, is more important to your customer than your company's name.

Generic Names or Brand Name Domains?

A domain name that matches your brand name is very important. The very name that you use to advertise your product or service is the name that you will want for your domain, because that is the first thing that people will type in their *Internet browser*.

It is also the easiest thing for them to remember, and whatever is easily remembered, will be more likely to be typed in than an obscure domain name. So, if you specifically sell Dayora Widgets, then you should get a domain name that says so, instead of one that just says Widgets.

You could compromise and have a number of websites selling different things with appropriate domain names. For example, stainless-steel-widgets.com will mimic the keywords that the prospect has typed into the search engine and will significantly improve the chances of that potential customer clicking on your website.

This approach has many advantages, including a higher search engine ranking, but due to the extra cost of registering multiple domain names can be an unjustifiably expensive strategy. You'll have to experiment to decide which domain name strategy is best for you.

Long or Short Domain Names?

Domain names can be of any length up to 67 characters. However, there appears to be some disagreement about whether a long or short domain name is better. Some argue that shorter domain names are easier to remember, easier to type and far less susceptible to mistakes: for example, "buyit.com" is easier to remember and less prone to typos than "buyitonmywebsitenow.com".

Others argue that a longer domain name is usually easier on the human memory - for example, "gywh.com" is a sequence of unrelated letters that is difficult to remember and type correctly, whereas if we expand it to its long form, "GetYourWidgetsHere.com", we are more likely to remember the domain name.

Due to the enormous numbers of domain names out there, it's increasingly difficult to get short meaningful domain names. If you manage to get a short domain name though, the key is to make sure it's a meaningful combination of characters and not some obscure initials.

As mentioned previously, long domain names that have your website's *keywords* in them also do better in a number of search engines since search engines give preference to keywords that are also found in a domain name.

All this said, go for a shorter name if you can get a meaningful one. If you can't, avoid the really long ones that verge on the 67 characters so that your customers don't feel it is a chore to type it in or commit it to memory.

Hyphenated-Names?

Should you get a hyphenated name?

Disadvantages:

1. It's easy to forget the hyphens when typing a name. Many users are used to typing things BuyWidgetsHere.com but

not buy-widgets-here.com. They'll probably leave out the hyphens and wind up at your competitor's site.

2. When people recommend your site to their friends verbally, having hyphens in your domain name leads to more potential errors than when the name does not contain hyphens. For example, how do you think your visitors will refer to your site if it is named "buy-widgets-here.com"? They might say, "I visited Buy Widgets Here dot com yesterday and it was great! When the friends go to the site, they don't type in the hyphens.

3. It is difficult to type. The hyphen key on the keyboard is just not an easy one to use. Even proficient typists often do not have a good grasp of the symbols.

Advantages:

1. Search engines can distinguish your keywords better and thus return your site more prominently in search results for those keywords occurring in your domain name.

2. The non-hyphenated form may no longer be available. At least this way, you still get the domain name you want.

Plurals, "The", and "My" Forms of the Domain Name

Very often, if you can't get the domain name you want, the *domain name registrar* will suggest alternate forms of the name you typed. For example, if you wanted widget.com, and it was taken (of course, it is), it might suggest formats such as:

- thewidget.com
- mywidget.com

- widgets.com

If you take the "the..." and "my..." forms of the domain name, you must always remember to promote your site with the full form of the name. Taking the plural can be more risky because it is easy to forget the "s".

COM, ORG, NET, etc?

If you get a domain name with an extension other than ".com", make sure that you promote your business or website with the full domain name. For example, if your domain name is "BuyWidgetsHere.net", make sure that when you advertise your site or business, call it "BuyWidgetsHere.net" not "BuyWidgetsHere". Otherwise people will assume a ".com" extension and go to the wrong place.

Registration Overview

Getting a domain name involves registering the name you want with an organization called InterNIC through a domain name registrar. For example, if you choose a name like "widgets.com", you will have to use a registrar and pay a registration fee that ranges from $10 to $35 for that name. That will give you the right to the name for between one and ten years, and you will have to renew it at the end of that period for the same amount.

It is best to register the name yourself, so you can be sure to be registered as the owner, the administrative and technical contact. Being the owner is vital - if a web host is listed as the owner, that web host can always decide to charge you for the use of the name later, and there is little you can do.

Although many web hosts suggest that you record them as the technical contact, you may prefer to keep yourself as one, so that when you want to transfer your name to a new web host, you don't have to wait for your old host to approve the transfer.

If you want to register a domain name, here's what you do:

1. Think of a few good domain names that you'd like to use.

2. Obtain from your web host the *DNS IP addresses* and names of their *primary and secondary nameservers*. Don't worry if you don't understand what these things mean, just save the information somewhere. The information can usually be obtained from their FAQs or other documentation on their website, usually under a category such as "domain name" or "DNS" or "domain name transfer." If you can't find it, email their webmaster. If you don't have a web host yet, all is not lost. Read on.

3. Get your credit card ready. This is a requirement of most if not all registrars. It will allow you to claim and get the domain name immediately on application. This is not an option (unfortunately).

4. If you already have a web host, you can just go to one of the registrars listed overleaf and apply for the domain name. Make sure you have the information mentioned in step 2.

5. If you do not have a web host, you can always use one of the registrars listed overleaf that allow you to park your domain name (usually free of hosting fees) at a temporary website specially set up for you. This way you can quickly secure your domain name and still take your time to set up the other aspects of your site.

List of Domain Name Registrars

There are numerous domain name registrars; below are just a few.

GoDaddy

This extremely popular registrar offers .com domain names for $9.99 per year or $6.99 if you transfer from another registrar. They have a web interface to manage your domains, free web redirection (where people who visit your domain will get transferred to another URL of your choice), free starter web page, free parked page or free "for sale" page, and an optional private domain registration where your domain is registered in the name of a proxy company. They offer .com, .us, .biz, .info, .net, .org, .ws, .name, .tv, .co.uk, .me.uk and .org.uk.

PLATE 29: WWW.GODADDY.COM

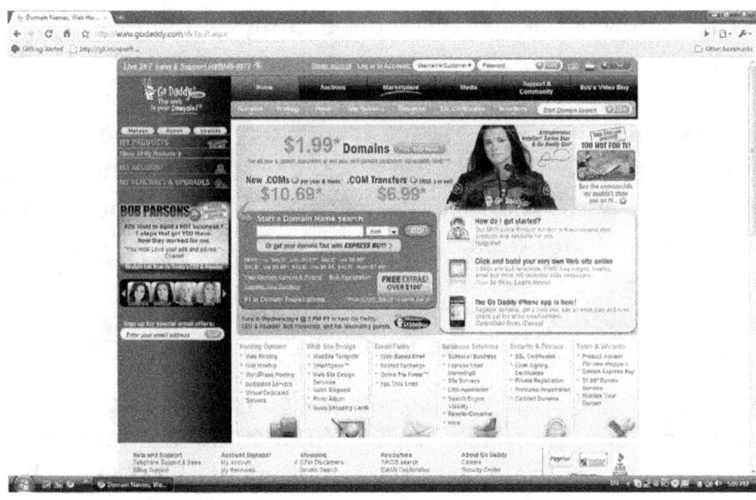

DOTSTER

This fairly popular registrar provides reasonably priced domain prices ($15.25 per domain), a convenient web interface to manage your domains, an optional privacy facility where your domain name is registered in the name of a proxy company, etc. They offer .com, .net, .org, .biz, .info, .us, .ca, .tv, .name, .cc, .de, .sr, .md, .co.uk, .us.com domains, etc. If you're transferring a domain here from other registrars, the price is even cheaper ($8.95).

REGISTER.COM

This well-established registrar currently sell domains for $35 per year or $79 for 3 years. They offer .com, .net, .bus, .us, .cn, .com.cn, .net.cn, .org.cn, .mobi, .info, .co.uk, .org.uk, .tv, .ws, .ca, .eu, .cc, .jp, .de, .co.nz, .net.nz, .org.nz, .tw, .com.tw, and .org.tw.

MONIKER

Prices for domain names differ, depending on the extension. For example, they charge $10.49 for .com, $6.04 for .net, $10.95 for .org, $5.49 for .info, etc. Their web interface allows you to manage matters pertaining to your domain, such as DNS, web forwarding (where you forward visitors to your domain to another URL of your choice), etc. You also have the option to add "Whois privacy", where your domain is registered in the name of a proxy company.

1&1 INTERNET

This is primarily a large web host that also provides domain name registrations. For .com, .org, .net, .info, .biz, .name domains, you are charged $6.99. They also offer .us domains for $2.99. The fee includes private domain registration, which means that your particulars are hidden from public view by registering it in the name of a proxy company. You also get a free email account, DNS management, domain forwarding and masking, and a starter website with each domain.

Note: A number of commercial web hosts will give you a free domain name if your website is hosted with them.

State Registration

Once you have a name for your company, you will want to register that name in your state. This will keep someone else from choosing and using the same name.

PLATE 30: WWW.STATELOCALGOV.NET

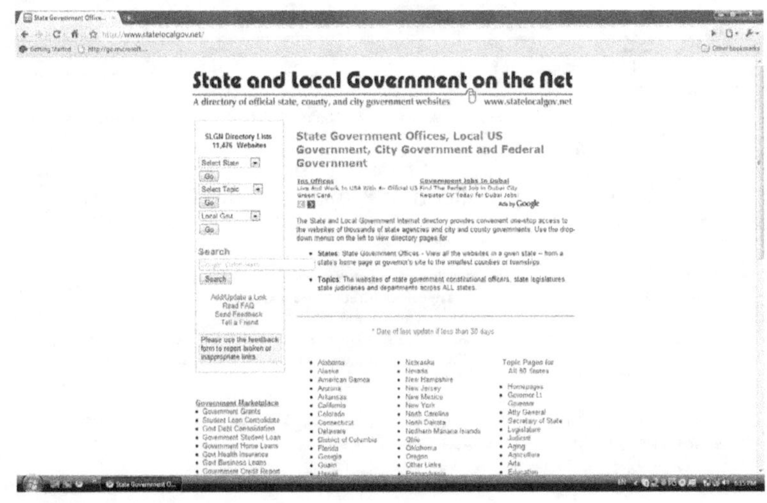

If you are going to do business under a name other than your personal name, you will need to check with your state's Attorney General's office to see if you need to register. You can find these offices online. These websites provide a good deal of information concerning how to register a company name. If you need help finding this office, visit the State and Local Government website at www.statelocalgov.net.

You might also want to trademark your name to protect it. You can trademark on a national or statewide level. To register your business as a local trademark, contact the Secretary of State's office in your area. To register as a national trademark, you will need to contact the U.S. Patent and Trademark Office (www.uspto.gov).

They also have a search engine (Trademark Electronic Search System, or TESS) that can help you determine if the name has already been trademarked.

PLATE 31: IP PROTECTION

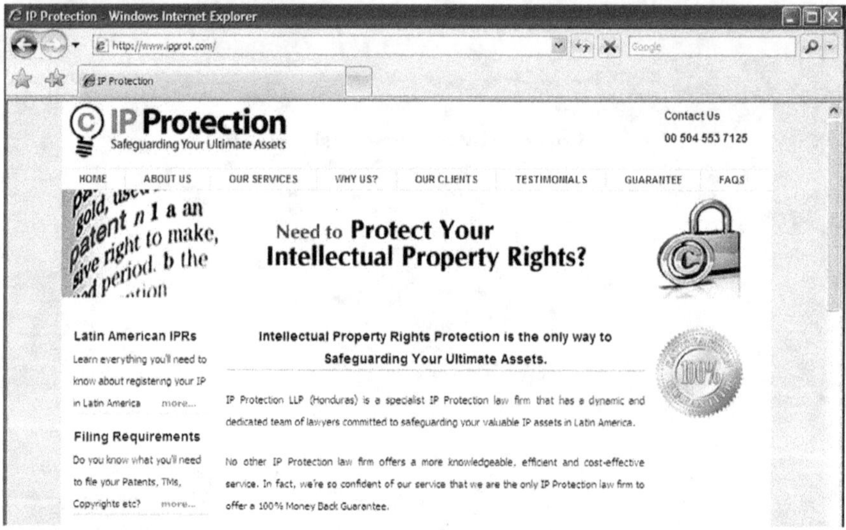

Companies, such as IP Protection (ipprot.com), will register your trademark for you for a reasonable price (as low as $500).

If, for whatever reason, you want a domain name with an unusual suffix, such as .it or .tv, then you will have to go directly to the vendor that sells those specific suffixes.

8

The Legal End of Business

Getting your business legally squared away is imperative to its operation and to your liability. Much of the legal information you'll require to start a business is accessible online.

Choosing a Legal Entity

Determining what legal form your business should take is one of the first questions you have to answer when starting your business. There is no right or wrong answer. The key is to understand the available options and determine what best fits your needs.

There are four main ways that you can organize your business:

- Sole proprietorship
- Partnership
- Corporation
- Limited Liability Company

Each has its own set of advantages and disadvantages.

SOLE PROPRIETORSHIP

A *sole proprietorship* is a business which is owned wholly and completely by a single individual. That individual is solely responsible for all aspects of the business and is personally *liable* for all debts, even those in excess of the amount invested in the business. The advantages of a sole proprietorship include:

- Low organizational and administrative costs
- Greatest freedom from government regulation
- Possible tax advantages (taxation of owner at his/her individual rate, owner may deduct losses from his/her own individual return)
- Minimal working *capital*

The disadvantages include:

- Unlimited liability
- Difficulty in raising capital (must use own money or borrow)

PARTNERSHIP

A *partnership* is a business jointly owned by two or more individuals. Each of the individuals is personally liable for the debts of the partnership. In some respects, the law treats a partnership as a legal entity, but in others, it does not. The rights and privileges of the partners and the partnership are defined by law and the partnership agreement.

The advantages to a partnership are similar to a sole proprietorship. One additional benefit is that a partnership allows for additional capital and management resources since more than one person is contributing to the company. In addition to the disadvantages of a sole proprietorship, a partnership also has the issue of divided authority.

CORPORATION

A *corporation* is a separate legal entity that acts as a single person and is created under statutory law. The corporation owns the business and, in turn, the corporation issues shares of stock to individuals investing in the corporation.

Corporations deliver two huge benefits to business owners. One benefit is a legal benefit and the other is a tax benefit.

Benefit One: Limited Liability

The big legal benefit that corporations provide business owners with is *liability protection*. What this means, practically speaking, is that the business owners are not liable for the debts of the business merely by virtue of their ownership.

However, to best understand what this limited liability protection means, you need to consider the situation that exists with respect to businesses that are un-incorporated.

In a sole proprietorship, for example, the proprietor is responsible for all the debts of the business. If the business signs a contract with some customer or vendor and then breaches the contract, or if the business fails to deliver on a financial promise made to some employee, the owner is liable.

A business organized as a general partnership works the same way. If the business breaches a contract, or makes and then breaks a financial promise, the partners in the partnership are liable.

In comparison, with a corporation, an owner (called a *stockholder or shareholder*) is not held liable.

Consider what this means for a small business. In a worst case scenario, outside creditors (these outside creditors would obviously include people such as the bank and vendors but might also include other people or organizations that you owe money to, such as customers and employees) might be able to strip the corporation of all its assets to pay a debt or force the corporation to liquidate to pay its debts. But these outside creditors would not be able to look to the corporation's owners for repayment merely because they own the corporation. Therefore, the legal liability protection provided by a corporation can be extremely valuable.

If you're concerned about the asset protection features of setting up and operating a corporation, get an attorney involved in your business or investment planning regularly. An attorney knowledgeable in business law can help you increase the liability protection that you gain from using a corporation for your business or investing.

Benefit Two: Potential Tax Savings

A second benefit of corporations relates to the income and payroll taxes that a business pays or that investors pay. As a general rule, small business corporations provide two tax benefits to their owners.

The first potential tax saving associated with incorporating your business applies to what the tax laws call a C corporation. A C corporation (but not an S corporation which will be discussed next) can typically provide tax-free fringe benefits to all of its employees.

In other words, the corporation can provide benefits such as medical insurance, reimbursement of medical expenses, a modest amount of life insurance, employee housing (in some cases), and so on. And this is true even if the only employee is a shareholder.

The cost of these benefits generally counts as business deductions for the corporation as long as the corporation doesn't discriminate in favor of shareholders and as long as the expenses are "ordinary and necessary" business expenses or expressly authorized as deductions by tax laws. But—and here's the neat thing—the deductions aren't taxed to employees.

Tax-free fringe benefits, then, allow a small corporation's owners to enjoy some of their business profits tax-free. In a situation where a one-employee-one-shareholder corporation provides full health benefits and housing to its single shareholder-employee, the corporation might be providing $20,000 or $30,000 a year in tax-free fringe benefits to that employee.

Yet those benefits, while allowing tax deductions for the corporation, would not be taxable to the employee. And this would mean that the annual tax savings would very likely run between $5,000 and $10,000 each year.

A corporation also affords its owners a second potential tax saving opportunity, *Subchapter S* status. To understand this benefit, though, you need to understand a thing or two about the payroll taxes that self-employed people (like sole proprietors and partners in partnerships) pay and that regular C corporations and their employees pay.

In a nutshell, money that a business owner makes in an active trade or business is not subject just to income taxes. In addition to income tax, each business owner also pays an employment tax equal to roughly 15% on the first $100,000 of profit and then roughly 3% on any profit above $100,000.

In the case of a sole proprietorship or partners in a partnership, the *employment taxes* are called self-employment taxes. In the case of a shareholder-employee in a corporation, the employment taxes are called Social Security and Medicare taxes.

To show you how the employment taxes work, suppose a sole proprietor, a partner in a partnership, or a single shareholder in a regular corporation (called a C corporation by tax laws) makes $200,000 in a year.

This proprietor or partner will pay roughly $15,000 in tax on the first $100,000 of business profit, and he or she will pay roughly $3,000 on the second $100,000 of profit.

If the single shareholder-employee extracts all of the $200,000 in corporate profit as salary—and this would probably be the most common approach for a small business—the shareholder (either directly or indirectly) also pays roughly $15,000 in tax on the first $100,000 of business profit and $3,000 on the second $100,000 of profit.

In all three of these cases, the business owner pays roughly $18,000 of employment taxes. Again, note that these employment taxes are in addition to the income taxes he or she pays on the

$200,000 of business profit. (Those income taxes probably total another $30,000 or $40,000.)

Things work differently if the corporation elects to be treated as a Subchapter S, or S corporation. In this case, the corporation probably sets the shareholder-employee's wages to a low but reasonable level. Perhaps this means wages equal to $60,000 annually. In this case, the employment tax equals 15% of only the $60,000 in wages, or $9,000.

As compared to the case where the same business makes $200,000 a year but is operated as a sole proprietorship, a partnership or a C corporation, an S corporation saves the shareholder-employee roughly $9,000 annually.

The Drawbacks of the Corporation

When you consider the benefits of a corporation—limited business liability and tremendous potential tax savings—you seemingly have almost the perfect business entity choice. So an obvious question is "Why wouldn't everyone become a corporation?"

Perhaps predictably, there are costs and headaches associated with incorporating.

As a general rule, a corporation increases the complexity and workload of administering your business. This increase in administrative complexity adds to your costs and your work.

1. For starters, a corporation will probably increase your banking, accounting, and insurance costs. For example, while the bank account for a sole proprietorship or informal partnership may be free if you keep a large-enough balance, the bank account for a corporation probably won't be free. The bank may charge $10, $20, or even more each month. The accountant and insurance company may, similarly, increase the prices they charge you.

2. Another increase in administrative complexity is that the corporation will need to do quarterly and annual payroll tax accounting — even if the only employee is the owner.

3. Related to this point, making an owner a corporate employee results in a new, extra payroll tax (*Federal Unemployment Tax*). This tax equals as much as 6.2% of the first $7,000 an employer pays individual employees in wages, or $434 per employee.

4. While a sole proprietorship or informal real estate partnership may be able to keep its *bookkeeping* and income tax return preparation very simple, a corporation needs to file its own tax return. And this tax return may cost anywhere from a few hundred dollars to a few thousand dollars annually.

5. A corporation may involve several hundred or even a few thousand dollars of startup expense. For example, you may spend money on publications like this. You may buy the services of accountants and attorneys. You will need to print new letterhead, business cards, and envelopes (if you use these) that use the new corporation's name in order to show the world that you're now operating as a corporation.

6. Finally, a corporation will mean that you need to have a *board of directors* (which will need to meet regularly, such as monthly, quarterly or annually) and annual stockholders meetings. You'll also need to keep good minutes of these meetings. And you will need to comply with either your corporate by-laws or state law as far as giving directors and shareholders advance notice of these meetings.

Typically, the incorporation option is uneconomical for very small businesses. On the other hand, any business that's producing profits that equal or exceed what the owner would earn if he or she worked as an employee for someone else probably should operate as a corporation or as a limited liability company.

In these cases, the corporation economically reduces business risk. As an added bonus, a C corporation can often produce tax savings to the business owner because shareholder-employers can get tax-free fringe benefits. Or alternatively, an S corporation can often save the owners thousands of dollars a year in income or payroll taxes.

LIMITED LIABILITY COMPANY

The last category is the Limited Liability Company. When all requirements are fulfilled, a Limited Liability Company (LLC) is taxed as a partnership, instead of a corporation, for federal tax purposes.

However, in contrast to a partnership, an LLC may allow its owners to be involved in the management of the business without exposure to personal liability. An LLC allows you to have limited liability, reduced organizational costs, relaxed regulation, and flexible allocation of income/expenses.

Research

You can do the research yourself to make determinations about the best way for you to organize your business. Talking with other small business owners to gain insight from their experiences is highly recommended. These small business owners will also be helpful in leading you to reputable bookkeepers, lawyers, or accountants, if you find yourself in need of those services.

Getting an Employer Identification Number

An *Employer Identification Number* (EIN) is also known as a Federal Tax Identification Number, and is used to identify a business entity. Generally, businesses need an EIN. The process for determining if your business needs an EIN is complicated. Below is how you can determine whether or not you need an EIN number:

If you are the **sole proprietor** of a company, you will need an EIN if any of the following statements are true:

- You are subject to a bankruptcy proceeding
- You have incorporated your company
- You have taken in partners and operate as a partnership
- You purchased or inherited an existing business that you operate as a sole proprietorship

You will not be required to obtain a new EIN if any of the following statements are true:

- You have changed the name of your business
- You have changed your location and/or add other locations
- You operate multiple businesses

If you choose a **corporation** status, you will be required to get an EIN if any of the following statements are true:

- Your corporation receives a new charter from the secretary of state
- You are a subsidiary of a corporation using the parent company's EIN or you become a subsidiary of a corporation
- You changed to a partnership or a sole proprietorship

- A new corporation is created after a statutory merger

You will not be required to obtain a new EIN if any of the following statements are true.

- You are a division of a corporation
- The surviving corporation uses the existing EIN after a corporate merger
- Your corporation declares bankruptcy
- Your corporate name or location changes
- Your corporation chooses to be taxed as an S corporation
- Reorganization of your corporation changes only the identity or place of business

To apply for an EIN, you will need to prepare and submit an IRS form, called the *SS-4*. Fortunately, you can fill out and submit an SS-4 online using the URL provided below:

https://sa1.www4.irs.gov/sa_vign/newFormSS4.do

COMPLETING AN SS-4 FORM

To complete the online *SS-4 form* or the paper SS-4 form carefully follow these steps:

1. Identify the *legal name* of your new company. You enter the new full legal name of your company into box 1.

2. Identify the trade name if that name differs from the legal name. As the form indicates, you enter the trade name of the business into box 2 if your trade name differs from the legal name.

3. Provide the firm's address. You enter the mailing address information into boxes 4a and 4b. If the business's street address differs from the mailing address, you also need to enter the street address into boxes 5a and 5b.

4. Identify the county and state of the new business. For example, if the county is Anycounty County, you enter Anycounty into the County box of box 6 and then enter your state into the State box.

5. Identify yourself. To do this, enter your full name into box 7a. Then, enter your *social security number*, individual taxpayer identification number, or EIN, into box 7b.

6. Identify your business entity. If you have chosen an LLC, in box 8a, mark the "Other" box. Enter "single member LLC" if your LLC has one owner.

7. Explain why you need an EIN. Mark one of the buttons in box 9 to indicate the reason you are requesting the EIN. For example, if you have just set up an LLC for a new business, you can mark the "Started New Business" button. You might also mark the "Other" business and then enter "LLC formation" into the blank box provided. If you indicate you are starting a business, briefly describe the type of business using the space provided.

8. Indicate when business activity started. Using box 10 of the SS-4, indicate when your business started using the month, day, and year from drop-down list boxes.

9. Identify the last month of the accounting year using box 11. In most cases, an accounting year ends in December. This is what you will enter into box 11 unless you are selecting a month other than December.

10. Indicate when you first paid or will first pay wages using the drop-down list boxes in box 12. For example, if you first paid or will first pay wages January 1, 2010, you enter JAN 1, and 2010.

11. Use box 13 to indicate how many employees you plan to have. Alternatively, if you do not expect to have employees, enter a 0 into the Agriculture, Household, and Other boxes.

12. Describe (at least in a general way) the principal activity of your new business using box 14.

13. Describe what you sell. Use box 15 to describe the principal product or service provided.

14. Indicate whether you have previously applied for an EIN. You can do this by marking either the 'Yes' or 'No' box in box 16a. If you indicate that you have applied for an EIN before, fill in the blanks in box 16b with the old entity's legal and trade name. Then, if possible, use box 16c to specify when you previously applied for the EIN, the city and state where you applied, and the actual EIN.

15. Submit the SS-4 form to the IRS. If you are using the online version of the SS-4 form, you simply click the 'Next' button to submit the SS-4 to the IRS. The IRS server then validates the SS-4 form you have filled out.

If the IRS server finds an error, it re-displays the form with red messages describing the error. You need to fix the error and click the 'Next' button again. If the IRS server does not find any errors, it gives you a preliminary EIN number.

Print the web page that provides the EIN for your records. Additionally, scroll down the page to the hyperlink that says "click here to print a completed version of the SS-4" form. Following the on-screen instructions, print a copy of the completed SS-4 form.

If you've prepared a paper version of the SS-4 form you can mail or fax it to the following address or fax number:

> Attn: EIN Operation
> Philadelphia, PA 19255
> Fax-TIN: 859-669-5760

PLATE 32: WWW.IRS.GOV

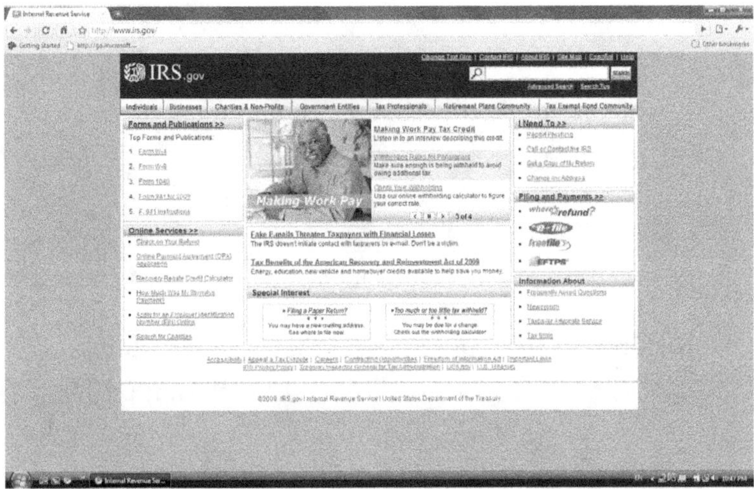

City Business License

Your city and your county may require a permit to operate your business. To find out if a license is needed, you can search on the Internet using your county name and state.

For example, if you type "your county your city local government" into a search engine, you will be directed to the information needed for setting up your business. You can also call your city or county's local government office and they will be able to assist you. You might find that a license is not required.

"Risk comes from not knowing what you're doing."

Warren Buffet

9

Business Plan

For any startup company there is one business tool that is often crucial to its success; the *business plan*. This document is a blueprint and road map for the structure, strategy, processes and growth of the business.

Researched, written and formatted correctly, the business plan can help ensure the success of any business by helping you to:

- Stick to your plan
- Outline your business model
- Identify future cash flow problems
- Secure funding

Another value of creating a business plan lies in the process of researching and analyzing your business in a systematic way. This act of planning helps you to think things through thoroughly, as well as studying and researching related facts and figures about your business. This process will help you assess ideas critically. It may take time now, but will help you avoid costly mistakes later.

Business plans are used to:

- Secure venture capital
- Assist public offerings
- Help coordinate a corporation's operational plans

- Help raise funding
- Coordinate a Total Quality Management (TQM) strategy
- Coordinate Management by Objectives (MBO) strategies
- Help a company's strategic planning

When you present your business plan to investors or bankers you will need to pay particular attention to your writing style, as you will be judged by the quality and appearance of your work as well as by your ideas and, most of all, whether the figures add up.

There are several different business plan formats that suit different purposes and should be formatted to suit the reader and the context of its presentation. It's not uncommon for businesses, especially start-ups, to have three or four formats for the same business plan:

- **An "elevator pitch"** is a three-minute summary of a business plan's executive summary. This is often used to whet the appetite of a potential investor in the hope that they will be interested enough to read the full plan.

- **A Printed Presentation for External Stakeholders** - a comprehensively-detailed, well-written, and correctly formatted plan targeted at external stakeholders.

- **An Internal Operational Plan** - a detailed document describing the planning strategies that may be required by management but may not be of interest to external stakeholders. Consequently, such plans have a somewhat higher degree of candor and informality than the version targeted at external stakeholders.

- **Slide Show/Oral Presentation** - a slide show and oral narrative that is meant to trigger discussion and interest potential investors to read the written plan. The content of the presentation is usually limited to the executive summary and a few key graphs showing financial trends and key decision making benchmarks. A demonstration of the product may also be included.

Individual investors often prefer a short, succinct plan that emphasizes the executive summary, whereas banks are mostly concerned about defaults, so a business plan for a bank loan should build a convincing case for your company's ability to repay the loan.

Venture capitalists are primarily concerned about initial investment, feasibility, and exit strategy/valuation. A business plan for a project requiring equity financing should explain why current resources, as well as future growth opportunities, and sustainable competitive advantage, will lead to a high exit valuation.

Although there are many different ways of presenting business plans, most formats include the sections covered in this chapter. You can remove or swap each section to suit your needs.

Note: There is an example of a comprehensive Business Plan available to download absolutely free to purchasers of this book at www.riskeliminator.com/free_downloads

Disclosure

A non-disclosure agreement is usually included as standard with any business plan. This is intended to protect a new business' unique ideas, trade secrets, unpatented products etc. A printed non-disclosure agreement should be signed by the reader of your business plan before they read it.

An externally targeted business plan should list all legal concerns and financial liabilities that might negatively affect investors. Depending on the amount of funds being raised and the audience to whom the plan is presented, failure to do this may have severe legal consequences.

Most business plans are divided into four distinct sections:

1) Description of the business
2) Management
3) Marketing
4) Finances

A common format of a business plan is as follows:

- Executive Summary
- Company Summary
- Products and Services
- Market Analysis
- Website
- Marketing Plan
- Financial Plan

These sections are outlined in more detail below.

Executive Summary

The Executive Summary is an overview of the whole plan and thus helps the reader quickly decide whether it is a good idea, and a viable business proposition. While it's the first section the reader will read, it should be the last section you should write; summarizing on information you used in the rest of the plan.

This section should be no more than one page long (preferably one paragraph), so make it enthusiastic, professional, complete, and concise. It should include everything that you would cover in a three-minute interview. Use the questions below to help you write the company description.

The *Executive Summary* should include summaries of:

- What is your business?
- What is your mission statement?
- What is your company's name?
- What are your company's products or services?
- To whom will you market your products or services? (State it briefly here—you will do a more thorough explanation in the *Marketing Plan* section).
- Who are you and why will you be good at this business?
- Who are your business' management team?
- What do you think the future holds for your business and your industry?
- Who are your competitors?
- Is the market growing?
- What changes do you foresee in the industry, short term and long term?
- How will your company be poised to take advantage of them?
- What is your exit strategy?

Describe your company's most important strengths and core competencies:

- What factors will make your business succeed?
- What do you think your major competitive strengths will be?
- Do you have a marketing or sales advantage?
- What background experience, skills, and strengths do you personally bring to this new venture?
- Do you have exceptional profitable financial projections?
- How profitable will your company be in 1, 3 and 5 years?
- What is your exit strategy?

The executive summary should also attempt at 'selling' the project; trying to persuade the reader that your business is a winner.

If applying for a loan, state clearly how much you want, precisely how you are going to use it, and how the money will make your business more profitable, thereby ensuring repayment.

The executive summary may have the following sub-sections:

- Mission Statement
- Company Vision
- Products/Services
- Market Analysis
- Business Model
- Key to Success
- Unique Selling Proposition (USP)
- Competitive Advantage
- Timetable

MISSION STATEMENT

Many companies have a brief *Mission Statement*, in 30 words or fewer, explaining their reason for being and their guiding principles, for example:

- Company Goals and Objectives
- Business Philosophy
- Your Business's Strengths and Core Competencies
- What is important to you in business?

Example of a Mission Statement:

"The Coca-Cola Company exists to benefit and refresh everyone it touches."

COMPANY VISION

Goals are destinations, where you want your business to be. Objectives are progress, markers along the way to your goals.

As you write your goals, you need to have a way to evaluate those goals. A good way to evaluate your goals is to determine if they are SMART goals:

S = Specific
M = Measurable
A = Attainable
R = Realistic
T = Timely

Specific – Goals should be straightforward and emphasize what you want to happen. Specifics help you focus your efforts and clearly define what you are going to do. A specific goal has a much greater chance of being accomplished than a general goal. To set a specific goal you must answer the six "W" questions:

Who: Who is involved?
What: What do I want to accomplish?
Where: Identify a location.
When: Establish a time frame.
Which: Identify requirements and constraints.
Why: Specific reasons, purposes, or benefits of accomplishing the goal.

A general goal would be, "The business will make money." But a specific goal would be, "The business will make $500,000 in the first year."

Measurable – If you cannot measure it, you cannot manage it. Establish concrete criteria for measuring progress toward the attainment of each goal you set. When you measure your progress, you stay on track, reach your target dates, and experience the exhilaration of achievement that spurs you on to continued effort required to reach your goal.

To determine if your goal is measurable, ask questions such as, 'How much? 'How many?' 'How will I know when it is accomplished?'

Attainable - When you identify goals that are important to you, you begin to figure out ways you can make them come true. You develop the attitudes, abilities, skills, and financial capacity to reach them. You begin seeing previously overlooked opportunities to bring yourself closer to the achievement of your goals.

Realistic - This is not a synonym for "easy." Realistic, in this case, means "do-able." To be realistic, a goal must represent an objective toward which you are both willing and able to work.

A goal can be both high and realistic; you are the only one who can decide just how high your goal should be. Be sure that every goal represents substantial progress.

Timely - A goal should be grounded within a time frame. With no time frame tied to it, there is no sense of urgency.

PRODUCTS/SERVICES

List all of your major services. For each service:

- Describe the most important features. What is special about it?
- Describe the benefits. That is, what will the product or service do for the customer?
- Evaluate the current and predicted demand for your products or services?
- Describe in depth the products or services you will offer.

- What factors will give you competitive advantages or disadvantages?
- What are the pricing, fee, or leasing structures of your products or services?

MARKET ANALYSIS

Outline exactly what you have done to research and analyze the market you intend entering and provide a breakdown of statistics, such as the current and predicted size of the market as well as any factors that your analysis has led you to believe that this is a good market to be in.

There are a number of analysis models that can help you analyze your prospective market. Below are three of the most popular and useful:

1. SWOT Analysis
2. Porter's Five Force Model
3. STEP Analysis

SWOT Analysis

A SWOT Analysis is broken down into four areas of analysis:

1. Strengths
2. Weaknesses
3. Opportunities
4. Threats
   (From this analysis you can identify your 'critical risks')

Strengths

- Advantages of proposition?
- Capabilities?

- Competitive advantages?
- USPs (unique selling points)?
- Resources, assets, people?
- Experience, knowledge, data?
- Financial reserves, likely returns?
- Marketing - reach, distribution, awareness?
- Innovative aspects?
- Location and geographical?
- Price, value, quality?
- Accreditations, qualifications, certifications?
- Processes, systems, IT, communications?
- Cultural, attitudinal, behavioral?
- Management cover, succession?
- Philosophy and values?

Weaknesses

- Disadvantages of proposition?
- Gaps in capabilities?
- Lack of competitive strength?
- Reputation, presence and reach?
- Financials?
- Own known vulnerabilities?
- Timescales, deadlines and pressures?
- Cash flow, start-up cash-drain?
- Continuity, supply chain robustness?
- Effects on core activities, distraction?
- Reliability of data, plan predictability?
- Morale, commitment, leadership?
- Accreditations, etc?
- Processes and systems, etc?
- Management cover, succession?

Opportunities

- Market developments?
- Competitors' vulnerabilities or new USPs?
- Industry or lifestyle trends?
- Technology development and innovation?
- Global influences?
- New markets, vertical, horizontal?
- Niche target markets?
- Geographical, export, import?
- Tactics: e.g. surprise, major contracts?
- Business, product or service development?
- Information and research?
- Partnerships, agencies, distribution?
- Volumes, production, economies?
- Seasonal, weather, fashion influences?

Threats

- Political effects?
- Legislative effects?
- Environmental effects?
- IT developments?
- Competitor intentions - various?
- Market demand?
- New technologies, services, ideas?
- Vital contracts and partners?
- Sustaining internal capabilities?
- Obstacles faced?
- Insurmountable weaknesses?
- Loss of key staff?
- Sustainable financial backing?
- Economy - home, abroad?
- Seasonality, weather effects?

From the analysis conducted above, you should be able to accurately identify the critical risks your specific business might face.

Porter's Five Force Model

Porter's model is a strategic tool used to identify whether new products, services or businesses have the potential to be profitable within a specific market.

> Force 1: The Degree of Rivalry
> Force 2: The Threat of Entry
> Force 3: The Threat of Substitutes
> Force 4: Buyer Power
> Force 5: Supplier Power

The Degree of Rivalry

- Number and size of firms
- Industry size and trends
- Fixed v variable cost bases
- Product or service ranges
- Differentiation, strategy

The Threat of Entry

- Entry ease/barriers
- Geographical factors
- Incumbents resistance
- New entrant strategy
- Routes to market

The Threat of Substitutes

- Alternatives price/quality
- Market distribution changes
- Fashion and trends
- Legislative effects

Buyer Power

- Buyer choice
- Buyers size/number
- Change cost/frequency
- Product or service importance
- Volumes, JIT scheduling

Supplier Power

- Brand reputation
- Geographical coverage
- Product or service level quality
- Relationships with customers
- Bidding processes/capabilities

Due to its limited assumptions, it's not advisable to develop a strategy based solely on Porter's model, but to analyze your market also using SWOT and STEP analysis models will help give a thorough analysis.

STEP Analysis

A STEP (or PEST) Analysis is an acronym for Social, Technological, Economic and Political factors, which are used to assess a commercial market. The STEP analysis headings are a framework for analyzing a marketing environment and can also, like SWOT analysis and Porter's Five Forces model, be used to review a strategy or position, the direction of a company, a marketing proposition, or an idea.

BUSINESS MODEL

Many experienced investors, especially venture capitalists, see themselves as investing in a business model as much as a specific company. Therefore, you should explain your business model succinctly so that it is easily understood. Later in the business plan (in the 'Company Summary' section) you will be able to explain it in more depth.

KEY TO SUCCESS

What's your key to success? The keys to success in your business may be any of the following:

- Quality of product or service
- Unique or superior quality service
- First-mover advantage
- Market share
- Profitable niche
- Lack of competition
- Expertise, experience or skills of management team
- Superior training
- Innovative, unique or more powerful technology
- Innovative, competitiveness or penetration of marketing
- High quality or depth of market research

UNIQUE SELLING PROPOSITION (USP)

A Unique Selling Proposition is nothing more than the thing that makes you different from your competitors. If you can identify it and leverage it, you should notice a difference in your customer base, your customer's satisfaction, and your bottom line.

A USP should have the following characteristics:

1. The proposition must be one that the competition either cannot, or does not, offer.

2. It must be unique; either a uniqueness of the brand or a benefit, service or offer not otherwise made in its specific market.

3. It must be so powerful that it can attract new customers to your product or service.

Examples of USPs include:

- Unique product or service
- Customized product or service
- Higher quality product or service
- Faster delivery or faster results
- Safer
- Simpler
- Lower cost
- More convenient
- Easier to use
- Less painful to use
- Easy payment schemes
- More for your customer's money
- Better customer service
- More choice
- Added value (e.g. a free complimentary product with it)

It's often an advantage to explain your USP, and how you're different, in your company's slogan. Here are some examples:

- Enterprise Rent-A-Car, "We'll pick you up."
- The Independent, "It is. Are you?"
- BMW, "The ultimate driving machine."
- British Airways, "The world's favorite airline."
- Burger King, "Have it your way."
- Federal Express, "When it absolutely, positively has to be there overnight."
- Heineken, "Heineken refreshes the parts other beers cannot reach."
- Avis, "We try harder."
- Wal-Mart, "Low prices, everyday."

How do you make a USP?

You can define your own USP by analyzing how you can provide something that your competitors don't provide. To do this you need to know:

1. Your customers
2. Your competition
3. Your company

Your Customers

You need to understand your customers' needs. Start by segmenting your market to determine exactly what they're looking for, what they love and hate, and how they spend their money. Then specifically fit your USP to your target customers.

Don't offer propositions that don't benefit your target market. If you're offering rapid turnaround times on your product or service but your customer base has all the time in the world, your USP is inappropriate.

Ideally, you want to identify what your clients are looking for and offer it to them. Consequently, your customers will remain loyal because they're getting from you what they can't get anywhere else.

Your Competition

Research what other companies are offering and either add something, or target a niche. Remember that the tighter the niche you sell to, the fewer competitors you'll have. Take advantage of that fact by identifying a very narrow group of people to sell to, thus eliminating more competition.

Yourself

Know what you can do, and what you can't do, and what you can't afford to do. Evaluate whether there's something you can do that your competition cannot. For example:

- Can you provide anything for free? Even a toll free phone call can make enough difference to get an order rather than your competitors.
- Can you provide overnight delivery while others do not? The extra expense you pay in delivery fees may be worth it if you have customers who need your product or service sooner.
- Can you provide a customized version of the product or service that you and your competition are selling? It could take a few extra dollars or minutes with each purchase, but the extra expense may be worthwhile when extra customers want something that fits their needs exactly.

COMPETITIVE ADVANTAGE

Does your company have unique skills, resources or strategies that your competitors can't implement as effectively? If so, this is a competitive advantage.

Understanding your competitive advantage is critical. It is the reason you are in business. It is what you do best that draws customers to buy your product or service instead of your competitor's.

Some successful companies deliberately make themselves unique and different in activities that they excel at and focus all of their energy in these areas. Sometimes called, "the lighthouse effect", this strategy deliberately makes the brand different from the others in a market to attract a niche segment of that market. Occasionally, these companies become cult brands, such as Apple, Harley Davidson, Linux etc., with a loyal customer base.

Once you have identified your competitive advantage(s), it is not enough just to have an advantage over your competitors. For your company to be great, your competitive advantage needs to be sustainable and able to endure the test of time, especially online where most advantages can be duplicated within a very short period of time:

- 99% of all new software or online facilities can be copied in days
- 70% of all new products are duplicated within one year
- 60% to 90% of process improvement is copied by competitors
- Competing on price is never sustainable
- Competing by 'being smarter' is never sustainable

"It is extremely dangerous to bet on the incompetence of your competitors".

Michael Porter

A sustainable competitive advantage is achieved by the following:

- Customers must see a consistent difference between your product or service and those of your competitor's.
- This difference needs to be obvious to your customers and it must influence their purchasing decision.
- Your competitive advantage must be difficult to imitate.
- Your competitive advantage must be constantly improved, nurtured, and worked at to maintain the edge over your competition.

TIMETABLE

Unless you can establish reasonable, achievable timetables for achieving your targets, it will be extremely difficult to calculate any required costs or resources. Investors and lenders will also require you to provide accurate time boxes, deadlines and agreed milestones to know whether they can expect a timely return on the money.

For shareholders and investors it is vitally important to reach or even succeed agreed milestones and targets as this will help your argument for raising more investment finance in the future.

Company Summary

The Company Summary section is an overview of the company and may have the following sub-sections:

- Company Ownership
- Legal Environment
- Proposed Location
- Key Personnel
- Personnel
- Objectives

- Business Model
- Management, Organization and Corporate structure
- Inventory
- Suppliers
- Credit Policies
- Pricing Strategy
- Sales Forecast
- Products and Services

COMPANY OWNERSHIP

Explain who owns the company and what format it will have.

- Is it a Sole Proprietor, Partnership, Corporation or Limited Liability Corporation (LLC)?
- Will it be an offshore company?
- Why have you selected this format?

LEGAL ENVIRONMENT

Describe the legal structure and environment in which the company is set.

- Licensing requirements
- Permits
- Health, workplace, or environmental regulations
- Zoning or building code requirements
- Insurance coverage
- Trademarks, copyrights, or patents (pending or existing)

PROPOSED LOCATION

Is the location of the business important to its success? Will you rent an office, work from home, a virtual office or use virtual network of distance workers working on outsourced jobs as and when required?

KEY PERSONNEL

If your business has any owners, shareholders or employees that are essential to the success of the business then you should mention them here.

- List exactly who are the key personnel of the business
- What is their experience, expertise, skill sets and how will they provide you with a competitive advantage?
- What is each person's relevant experience and background?
- What are their special areas of expertise?
- What is the education level of each key personnel?

If you plan to employ more than 10 employees it may be useful to add an organizational chart showing the management hierarchy and who is responsible for key functions.

Include the position description for each key employee. If you are planning to get a loan or find an investor, include resumés of owners and key employees.

Professional and Advisory Support

List the following:

- Board of directors
- Management advisory board
- Attorneys
- Accountants
- Insurance agents
- Banker
- Consultants

- Mentors and key advisors

PERSONNEL

Most business plan formats include one or more sub-sections for personnel.

If you have more than one key person, it's usually a good idea to include resumés for your key players in the Appendix section of your document, which comes at the end of the business plan.

Give an overview of all the personnel employed by your company.

- What is the optimum number of employees for your business?
- Where and how will you find the right employees?
- What will be the training methods and requirements?
- Do you require specific training?
- If so, what is it?
- Who does which tasks?
- Do you have written procedures prepared?
- Who will manage the business on a day-to-day basis?
- What experience does that person bring to the business?
- If you are managing the business, list your experience of doing so.
- What special or distinctive competencies do you possess?
- Do you have any professional or advisory support?
- For certain functions, will you use contract workers in addition to employees?
- Do you have cover should any employees be sick?
- What would happen if a member of staff left or became incapacitated?

OBJECTIVES

It is vital to set clear and specific objectives to provide you with a yardstick to measure your ability to achieve your vision. These are measurable targets that can help you achieve the mission of your business. You should include short, medium and long term objectives, stating where you see the company in 1, 3, 5 or 10 years time. These predictions should be included in the company's mission and vision statements.

Objectives relate to:
- Return on investment (ROI)
- Market position/share
- Projected stages of technological development
- Levels of financial performance

To be effective an objective should:
- Refer to a specific outcome not an activity
- Be measurable
- Be realistic
- Be achievable
- Be based on actual capabilities of the business
- Contain a specific time deadline

Example objectives:
- To generate $470,000 in sales by the end of the year one
- To achieve $250,000 in after tax profits in year one
- To increase inventory turnover from 10,000 units to 25,000 units during year two

BUSINESS MODEL

A Business Model is a description of the operations of a business, including the components, functions, revenues and expenses that the business generates. It may help to define your business model by using the following headings:

- Infrastructure
- Offering
- Customers
- Finances

Infrastructure

- Will you outsource any elements of the business model?
- If so, which elements will be outsourced?
- Will your core competences be kept in-house?
- What will be the company's distribution channel (the means by which you will deliver products and services to customers)?
- What is your operational plan (the daily operations of the business, its location, equipment, people, processes, and surrounding environment).

Offering

- What is your value proposition?
- What products and services will you offer?
- How does your company differentiate itself from its competitors? Why will customers buy from your company and not from another?
- What is your value configuration (the rationale which makes your business mutually beneficial for your business and your customers)?

Customers

- Who are your target customers?
- Can you break this target sector down further to market segments?

Finances

- How will your company make its revenue?
- How many revenue streams will your company use to generate its income?

Example Business Model:

The company will distribute all its digital cameras and complimentary products by post, through standard post or courier services. It will advertise its products exclusively through online advertising; targeted at underwater photography enthusiasts and professionals. The company's competitive advantage will be its extensive knowledge-base, extremely knowledgeable staff and outstanding customer service, as well as its competitive pricing.

MANAGEMENT, ORGANIZATION AND CORPORATE STRUCTURE

Explain the different levels and sections of your company's management and leadership structure. If you're a sole trader or a small start-up business then you may not need this section.

If your company is a large organization then you should detail the different layers of leadership and authority. If you have a multi-layered hierarchy to your corporate structure, adding a flow diagram can help the reader understand the company's chain of command.

INVENTORY

The cost of keeping stock and the system used to optimize the turnover of stock can have a huge influence on the overall operating costs of your business. In this section you should detail what, where and how your stock is managed.

- Will you keep stock?

- Will you only sell digital, downloadable products?
- Will you only resell other companies' products?
- Will you use a drop-shipping system?
- Will you combine various strategies, including your own inventory?
- What kind of inventory will you keep?
- What will be the average value of your stock?
- Where will your inventory be stored?

SUPPLIERS

The cost, availability and timely delivery of supplies, as well as the relationship with your suppliers, can also have an immense impact on the efficiency, trustworthiness, longevity and bottom line of your business. It would be useful to include the following details to your business plan:

- Identify key suppliers, including their names and addresses
- The type and amount of inventory supplied
- Your suppliers' credit and delivery policies
- Have you verified your suppliers?
- What is the history and reliability records of your suppliers?
- Are you at the mercy of wholesalers for your raw materials or product components?
- How can you manage suppliers and gain more buying power over them?
- Can you simplify your products and reduce your supply needs?
- Can you buy in bulk and store them somewhere in a cost-effective manner?
- Can you buy some things pre-fabricated cheaper than doing it yourself (or vice versa)?

CREDIT POLICIES

Here you should state whether or not you intend to use any credit policies and, if so, the details of those credit schemes.

- Do you plan to sell on credit?
- Do you really need to sell on credit? Is it customary in your industry and expected by your clientele?
- How will you check the creditworthiness of new applicants?
- What terms will you offer your customers; that is, how much credit and when is payment due?
- Do you know what it will cost you to extend credit? Have you built the costs into your prices?
- Do you plan to use a debt factoring company?

PRICING STRATEGY

The optimum pricing of your product or service could be crucial, and something that any potential investor will want to know, especially if they are expert in your industry.

- Explain your pricing strategy and the reasons for using that rather than others.
- Explain your method or methods of setting prices.
- Does your pricing strategy fit with what was revealed in your competitive analysis?
- Compare your prices with those of the competition. Are they higher, lower, the same? Why?
- How important is price as a competitive factor? Do your intended customers really make their decisions based mostly on price?

Note: For a detailed explanation of the most common pricing strategies and the rationale behind using specific pricing strategies to fit specific marketing strategies read, 'Fortune Cookie' by the same author.

SALES FORECAST

Now that you have described your services, customers, markets, and marketing plans in detail, it is time to attach some numbers to your plan.

You should now prepare a month-by-month projection called a *Sales Forecast*. The forecast should be based on your historical sales, the marketing strategies that you have just described, as well as your market research, and industry data, if available.

PLATE 33: SALES FORECAST

	A	B	C	D
1	SALES FORECAST			
2	Sales	Month 1	Month 2	Month 3
3	Products and Services	$12,000.00	$12,000.00	$14,000.00
4	Other	$27,000.00	$0.00	$0.00
5	Total Sales	$39,000.00	$12,000.00	$14,000.00
6	Direct Cost of Sales	Month 1	Month 2	Month 3
7	Overall Costs	$35,500.00	$5,550.00	$5,750.00
8	Other	$0.00	$0.00	$0.00
9	Total Costs	$35,500.00	$5,550.00	$5,750.00
10				
11	SALES FORECAST			
12	Sales	Year 1	Year 2	Year 3
13	Products	$190,000.00	$237,500.00	$296,875.00
14	Services	$27,000.00	$0.00	$0.00
15	Total Sales	$217,000.00	$237,500.00	$296,875.00
16	Direct Cost of Sales	Year 1	Year 2	Year 3
17	Overall Costs	$101,750.00	$80,250.00	$89,450.00
18	Other	$0.00	$0.00	$0.00
19	Total Costs	$101,750.00	$80,250.00	$89,450.00

You may want to do two forecasts:

- A "best guess", which is what you really expect.
- A "worst case" low estimate that you are confident you can reach no matter what happens.

Remember to keep notes on your research and your assumptions as you build this sales forecast. This is critical if you are going to present it to lenders or investors.

PRODUCTS AND SERVICES

List all of your major products and services. For each product or service answer these questions:

- Describe its important features. What is special about it?
- Describe the benefits. That is, what will the product or service do for the customer?
- What is the current and predicted demand for the product or service?
- Describe in depth the product or services you will offer.
- What factors will give you competitive advantages or disadvantages? Examples include level of quality or unique or proprietary features, etc.
- What are the pricing, fee, or leasing structures, of your product or service?
- Is the product or service you are selling complimentary to a different product or service?

Marketing Overview

In this section you should provide an overview of what your marketing campaign will consist of and why. For example:

- Market size and growth
- Your product or service
- Usage of your product or service
- Internet usage
- Targeted customer profile
- Competitor analysis
- Niche Identification
- Positioning
- Potential market
- Marketing strategy
- Distribution channels

MARKET SIZE AND GROWTH

What is the current and predicted size of your market and how did you acquire these figures?

PRODUCT/SERVICE USAGE

How many people use your product or service? Can you break down the usage figure into age, gender, geographic, economic or social segments? What percentage of this total market do you expect to sell to?

INTERNET USAGE

How many people use the Internet now and in the future? Which segment of Internet users are you targeting? How many potential users can you identify as potential customers?

TARGETED CUSTOMER AND PROFILE

Identify your target customers; their characteristics, their geographic locations, and socio-economic demographics. You may have more than one customer group. For each customer group, you can construct what is called a demographic profile:

- Age
- Gender
- Location
- Disposable income
- Other distinguishing characteristics

Segmentation

Where possible, try to break these demographics down into more usable 'segments' of data, such as 45-year-old ladies that read women's magazines etc. The more you can precisely segment your customers the more accurate and cost-effective your marketing will be.

COMPETITOR ANALYSIS AND COMPARISON

- What companies will compete with you? List your major competitors with their names and address.
- Will they compete with you across the board, just for certain services, certain customers, or in certain locations?
- Will you have significant indirect competitors?
- How will your services compare with the competition?

Use the *Competitive Analysis Table* to compare your company with your two most important competitors. In the first column are key competitive factors.

Table 1: Competitive Analysis

Factor	Me	Strength	Weakness	Competitor A	Competitor B	Importance to Customer
Services						
Price						
Quality						
Service						
Reliability						
Expertise						
Company Reputation						
Location						
Credit Policies						
Advertising						

In the column labeled "Me" state how you honestly think you will be evaluated in potential customers' minds. Then consider whether their opinion will be a strength or a weakness for you.

Then analyze each major competitor. In a few words, state how you think they compare. In the final column, estimate the importance of each competitive factor to the customer. 1 = critical; 5 = not very important.

Now, write a short paragraph stating your competitive advantages and disadvantages.

NICHE IDENTIFICATION

A market in its entirety is too broad in scope for any but the largest companies to tackle successfully. The best strategy for a smaller business is to divide demand into manageable market niches, then offer specialized goods and services attractive to a specific group of prospective buyers.

Now that you have systematically analyzed your industry, your services, your customers, and the competition, you should have a clear picture of where your business fits into the world.

In one short paragraph, define your niche, your unique corner of the market.

If you do target a new niche market, make sure that this niche does not conflict with your overall business plan. For example, a small company that makes unique, hand-made products can't survive in a market for inexpensive, mass-produced products, regardless of the demand.

POSITIONING

Where do your products or services fall in relation to the total market? Is this the optimum position you want?

To appeal directly to your target market, where in relation to your competition should you position your products or services? Are you going to 'stack 'em high and sell 'em cheap' or try to appeal to the high end consumer and sell a premium brand at a premium price?

Are you "all things to all people"? If you are truly "in the middle," you should regularly examine how well you're performing against competitors (with the help of a good accounting system); otherwise, you ought to revise your positioning strategy.

POTENTIAL MARKET

An accurate estimate of the total potential market size at launch and in the future is a very important statistic because it will give your stakeholders, lenders and investors an idea of the business' full potential and realistic expectations. Try to research the following statistics:

- Globally, how many people use your product or service?
- What is the total size of your market?
- What is the current demand for your product or service within your target market?
- What growth potential and opportunities exist for a business of your size?
- Do any barriers-to-entry exist in entering this market?
- If so, how will you overcome these barriers?
- How could a change in the economy affect your business?

MARKETING STRATEGY

Now outline a marketing strategy that is consistent with your niche and market positioning:

- How will you get the word out to customers?
- If you advertise, which media will you use and how often?
- Why this marketing mix and not some other?
- Have you identified low-cost methods to get the most out of your promotional budget?

Will you use methods other than paid advertising? Such as:

- Testimonials
- Word of Mouth
- Referral Programs
- Vendor's shows

- Writing Articles
- Newsletters
- Press Releases
- Radio and TV guest appearances

Image

- What image do you want to project?
- How do you want customers to see you?
- Are you employing a company to help you with your branding?

Promotional Budget

- How much will you spend on the promotions listed above?
- Before startup? (startup budget)
- Ongoing? (operating plan budget)

DISTRIBUTION CHANNELS

You will need to outline exactly how you intend selling and delivering your products or services:

- Is your product downloadable or will it need a courier service to deliver it?
- Do you have a backup or alternative method of delivery?
- Will you offer fast or free delivery?
- How can you get your products out to new outlets profitably?
- Are there unbranded or drop-shipping opportunities?
- Can you bundle in your products or services with someone else's?
- Can you partner with service providers?

PRODUCT/SERVICE

In the Executive Summary, you described your products and services as you see them. Now describe them from your customers' point of view, emphasizing in more detail the benefits to your customers.

- Product range
- Services offered
- Future products and services
- Complimentary products or services
- Up-selling and cross-selling opportunities

Website

Give an overview of the purpose and commercial aims of the website and how you will try to achieve those aims:

- Website features and facilities
- Online payment system
- Online security

WEBSITE FEATURES AND FACILITIES

Outline exactly how many features and facilities your website will have and explain and justify each one. For example:

- Customer/membership database
- Shopping cart
- Newsletter
- Blog/forum
- Email autoresponder
- Video, 3D, zoom etc. to demonstrate your product

ONLINE PAYMENT SYSTEM

Clarify how customers will pay for your product or service:

- Do you have a credit card processing system?
- If so, which financial institution provided the system?
- Do you have an online Merchant ID?
- If so, which financial institution provided the Merchant ID?
- Into which bank account will sales revenue be paid?
- What will be the yearly, monthly and transaction fees?

ONLINE SECURITY

Mention the security systems and features that are in place to protect your online business:

- Can you guarantee your website's continuous uptime?
- Have you taken every reasonable step to ensure the privacy of your customers' personal and financial information?
- What disaster recovery, data recovery and data backup procedures do you have in place?
- Do you have any firewalls, anti-virus or anti-hacking software, hardware or systems in place?
- Do you have any digital security certificates?

Marketing Plan

No matter how good your product or service, your venture will not succeed without effective marketing. This begins with careful, systematic research. It is dangerous to assume that you already know everything about your intended market. You need to do market research to make sure you are on track. If you use the business planning process as your opportunity to uncover data, and to question your marketing efforts, your time will be well-spent.

A marketing plan could include the following sections:

- Sales strategies
- Strategic alliances
- Online marketing strategies
- Offline marketing strategies

SALES STRATEGIES

Detail how you intend selling your products or services. Selling consists of two main functions: *tactics* and *strategy*.

Sales strategy is the planning of sales activities: methods of reaching clients, competitive differences and resources available.

Tactics involve the day-to-day selling: prospecting, sales process, and follow-up.

Sales strategies and tactics can create a competitive advantage, especially if you use several different strategies and tactics in a focused and coordinated manner. For example, you could separate your sales strategy into five major areas:

1. Online Sales Strategy
2. Direct Sales Force Strategy
3. Indirect Sales Channel Strategy
4. Sales Prospecting Strategy
5. Sales Campaign Strategy

Online Sales Strategy

Your online sales strategy includes all the devices you'll use to direct your online visitors to your pay page and, hopefully, turn them into customers.

- Sales copy
- Sales funnel
- Special offers
- Value-added offers
- Up-selling offers
- Cross-selling offers
- Product and service-specific landing pages etc.

The sales and visitor figures you will need to analyze the effectiveness of your online sales strategy can be automated in your website analytics, including your return on investment (ROI), advertising costs and conversion rates.

Direct Sales Force Strategy

This strategy allows a company to focus its resources, such as account managers and follow-up sales teams, and bonus them based on achievable and measurable goals.

- If you are going to have a sales force, do you plan to use internal, independent or outsourced representatives?
- How many salespeople will you recruit for your sales force?
- What type of recruitment strategies will you use?
- How will you train your sales force?
- What about compensation for your sales force?

You need to determine the average number of sales contacts (i.e. phone calls, emails etc.) you will need to make per sale, the average dollar size per sale, and the average dollar size per vendor.

Indirect Sales Channel Strategy

This strategy provides leverage to increase your sales success. For example, using affiliates, resellers, franchise partners and licensed partners.

Sales Prospecting Strategy

A Sales Prospecting Strategy will be supported by a direct sales force, indirect sales channels and supported by direct mail, banner and pay-per-click advertising, and search engine placement, to build your sales prospects list to a quality level. One strategy is to offer free e-books, digital products or newsletters to acquire e-mail addresses and contact details.

Sales Campaign Strategy

A Sales Campaign Strategy is designed to lay out a clear direction in which to maximize all resources at your disposal with clear campaign ideas, messages and target markets/customer groups.

STRATEGIC ALLIANCES

Do you intend to use partnerships, affiliate schemes, or any strategic alliances to help sell your major products and services? If so, who and why?

ONLINE MARKETING STRATEGIES

Here you should state exactly which online marketing strategies, tactics and campaigns you intend using. Below are just some of the strategies you will need to use:

- Search Engine Optimization (SEO)
- Sponsored links e.g. Pay Per Click (PPC) advertising
- Opt-in email advertising
- Community building: blogging and social networking
- Inward link-building

OFFLINE MARKETING STRATEGIES

Here, add any traditional marketing campaigns you intend running. For example:

- Television advertising
- Radio advertising
- Magazine and newspaper advertising
- Point-of-sale promotions in retail units etc.
- Posters, handouts, samples and leaflets
- Tradeshows and exhibitions

Note: Visit www.riskeliminator.com/free_downloads for a comprehensive list of every type of e-marketing that can be undertaken.

Financial Plan

Your Financial Plan should include most, if not all, of the following expenses, projections, and supporting documents:

- Expenses
- Financial Projections

- Supporting Documents

EXPENSES

You will have startup expenses before you even begin operating your business. It is important to estimate these expenses accurately and then to plan where you will get sufficient capital. This is a research project, and the more thorough your research efforts, the less chance that you will leave out important expenses or underestimate them.

Explain your research and how you arrived at your forecast of expenses. These expenses can include:

- Startup expenses
- Director's loans
- Loan applications
- Capital equipment and supply list

Start-up Expenses include:

- Cost of travel
- Trade shows
- Educational or training seminars
- Accounting and legal fees
- Consulting fees
- Building costs
- Supplies or materials needed to get your business started (not inventory or raw materials)
- Fees paid to obtain licenses
- Accounting or legal fees for formation of the entity

Here is also where you will want to think about keeping your *overhead expenses* low. Overhead expenses include three general areas: indirect materials, indirect labor, and all other miscellaneous production expenses, such as taxes, insurance, *depreciation*, supplies, utilities (e.g. electricity and gas), and repairs. In essence, overhead expense is part of the total costs of maintaining and staffing a business.

Reducing overheads is essential if you want to remain competitive. If your overhead is high, the price of your products or services will have to be higher without you making any more profit.

Keeping overheads low is not too difficult. For example:

- If possible, begin your business in your garage, basement, or back room
- Remember that you don't need the latest and greatest technology
- Upgrade selectively

You may need one new computer but not everyone in the office may need one. Determine upgrades by what needs to be done and by whom and whether current equipment can handle these functions (without having to upgrade anything else).

FINANCIAL PROJECTIONS

Here you should include all the financial projections you or an investor or lender would require to make accurate financial decisions. Financial projections should include:

- Profit and Loss Projection
- Cash Flow
- Balance Sheet(s)**
- Break-Even Analysis
- Personal Financial Statement

** Detail by month, first year. Detail by quarters, second and third years.

Together these projections constitute a reasonable estimate of your company's financial future. More important, the process of thinking through the financial plan will improve your insight into the inner financial workings of your company.

PLATE 34: PROFIT & LOSS PROJECTION

	IND. %	Oct-01	% B/A	Nov-01	%	Dec-01	%	Jan-02	%
1 Profit and Loss Projection (12 Months)									
2 Fiscal Year Begins									
3 Oct-01									
4 New Co. Limited									
5 **Revenue (Sales)**									
6 Nikon D3	18.0	2,000.00	16.7	2,000.00	16.7	2,000.00	14.3	2,000.00	16.7
7 Panasonic SDR	20.0	2,000.00	16.7	2,000.00	16.7	2,000.00	14.3	2,000.00	16.7
8 Pentax W30	20.0	2,000.00	16.7	2,000.00	16.7	3,000.00	21.4	2,000.00	16.7
9 Sanyo Xacti	22.0	2,000.00	16.7	2,000.00	16.7	3,000.00	21.4	2,000.00	16.7
10 Olympus SW	30.0	4,000.00	33.3	4,000.00	33.3	4,000.00	28.6	4,000.00	33.3
11 **Total Revenue**	100.0	12,000.00	100.0	12,000.00	100.0	14,000.00	100.0	12,000.00	100.0
12									
13 **Expenses**									
14 Running expenses		450.00		450.00		450.00		450.00	
15 Professional fees								250.00	
16 Wages		3,000.00		3,000.00		3,000.00		3,000.00	
17 Office equipment and furniture									

Profit and Loss Projection

A 12-month Profit and Loss Projection is where you put together all the numbers and get an idea of what it will take to make a profit. Your sales projections will come from a sales forecast in which you forecast total sales, cost of goods sold, expenses, and profit month-by-month for one financial year.

Profit projections should be accompanied by a narrative explaining the major assumptions used to estimate your company's income and expenses.

Cash Flow Projection

Cash is King - businesses fail because they cannot pay their bills. Every part of your business plan is important, but none of it means a thing if you run out of cash.

PLATE 35: CASH FLOW PROJECTION

CASHFLOW FORECAST New Co. Limited								
SALES AND INCOME	MONTH 1	MONTH 2	MONTH 3	MONTH 4	MONTH 5	MONTH 6	MONTH 7	MONTH 8
Sales	12,000	12,000	14,000	12,000	14,000	18,000	15,000	12,000
Capital	27,000	0	0	0	0	0	0	0
Other	0	0	0	0	0	0	0	0
TOTAL RECEIPTS	39,000	12,000	14,000	12,000	14,000	18,000	15,000	12,000
OUTGOINGS	MONTH 1	MONTH 2	MONTH 3	MONTH 4	MONTH 5	MONTH 6	MONTH 7	MONTH 8
Running of Premises	450	450	450	450	450	450	450	450
Professional Fees	0	0	0	250	0	0	0	250
Wages	3,000	3,000	3,000	3,000	3,000	3,000	3,000	3,000
Office Equipment/Furniture	27,000	0	0	0	0	100	0	0
Computers and Peripherals	1,500	0	0	0	0	0	0	0
Stationery and Printing	200	200	200	200	200	200	200	200
Advertising etc	200	200	200	200	200	200	200	200
Flyers	0	0	0	0	0	0	0	0
Marketing Gifts	0	0	0	0	0	0	0	0
Website Costs	1,500	50	50	50	50	50	50	50

The point of a *Cash Flow Projection* worksheet is to plan how much you need before startup; for preliminary expenses, operating expenses, and reserves. You should keep updating it and using it after launch, as it will enable you to foresee any cash flow shortages in time to do something about them (e.g. cut expenses, or negotiate a loan).

Essentially, the cash flow projection is just a forward look at your checking account. For each item, determine when you expect to receive cash (for sales) or when you will have to write a check (for expense items).

You should track essential operating data, which is not necessarily part of cash flow but allows you to track items that have a heavy impact on cash flow, such as sales and inventory purchases. Also, track cash outlays before opening in a pre-startup column. You will probably have already researched those for your startup expenses plan.

Your cash flow will show you whether your working capital is adequate. Clearly, if your projected cash balance ever goes negative, you will need more start-up capital.

Explain your major assumptions, especially those that make the cash flow differ from the *Profit and Loss Projection*. For example:

- If you make a sale in month one, when do you actually collect the cash? When you buy inventory or materials, do you pay in advance, upon delivery, or much later? How will this affect cash flow?
- Are some expenses payable in advance?
- If so, when?
- Are there irregular expenses, such as quarterly tax payments that should be budgeted?

Loan payments, equipment purchases, and owner's drawings do not show on profit and loss statements but definitely do take cash out. Be sure to include them. And of course, depreciation does not appear in the cash flow because you do not write a check for it.

PLATE 36: BALANCE SHEET

	Balance Sheet		
	New Co. Limited		Date: 30-09-2009
	Financial Year: 1Oct 2008 to 30 Sept 2009		
			(Amount in US $)
	Assets		**2009**
	Current assets		
		Cash	8,300.00
		Certificates of deposit	5,000.00
		Securities - stocks / bonds / mutual funds	20,000.00
		Accounts receivable	15,600.00
		Short-term investments	2,500.00
	Total current assets		**51,400.00**
	Fixed(long-term) assets		
		Property	149,100.00
		Office Equipment and furniture	28,500.00
	Total fixed assets		**177,600.00**

Balance Sheet

A balance sheet is one of the fundamental financial reports that any business needs for reporting and financial management. A balance sheet shows what items of value are held by the company (*assets*), and what its debts are (*liabilities*). When liabilities are subtracted from assets, the remainder is owners' equity.

Break-Even Analysis

A *Break-even Analysis* predicts the sales volume, at a given price, required to recover total costs. In other words, it is the sales level that is the dividing line between operating at a loss and operating at a profit.

PLATE 37: BREAK-EVEN ANALYSIS (UNIT SALES)

	A	B
1	**New Co Limited**	
3	**Break-even Point**	
4	Variable cost/unit	$ 29.34
5	Fixed cost	4,300.00
6	Price/unit	$ 257.45
7		
8	BEP unit	18.85
9	Break Even Point	$ 4,852.93

Expressed as a formula, break-even is:

Break-Even Sales = Fixed Costs / 1 – Variable Costs

(Where fixed costs are expressed in dollars, but variable costs are expressed as a percent of total sales.)

Note: Include all assumptions upon which your break-even calculation is based.

Personal Financial Statement

Include *personal financial statement*s for each owner and major stockholder, showing assets and liabilities held outside the business and *personal net worth*.

It's common for owners to draw on their own personal assets to finance the business, and these statements will show what is available to sustain the business. Bankers and investors will want to see this information as well.

PLATE 38: PERSONAL FINANCIAL STATEMENT

1	**Personal Financial Statement of: Dr Ben Black**	
2	**as of:** 30/09/2009	
3		
4	**Assets**	**Amount in Dollars**
5	Cash - checking accounts	$3,800.00
6	Cash - savings accounts	$4,500.00
7	Certificates of deposit	$5,000.00
8	Securities - stocks / bonds / mutual funds	$20,000.00
9	Accounts receivable	$15,600.00
10	Life insurance (cash surrender value)	$100,000.00
11	Personal property (autos, jewelry, etc.)	$149,100.00
12	Retirement Funds (eg. IRAs, 401k)	$400,000.00
13	Real estate (market value)	$275,000.00
14	*Total Assets*	**$973,000.00**

Note: Examples of all these financial projections are available free to all purchasers of this book at www.riskeliminator.com/free_downloads

SUPPORTING DOCUMENTS

Below is a list of various useful supporting documents. Include as many of these as you think are relevant or helpful.

- Tax returns of principals for last three years
- Personal financial statement (all banks have these forms)

- For franchised businesses, a copy of franchise contract supporting documents provided by the franchisor
- Copy of proposed lease or purchase agreement for building space
- Copy of licenses and other legal documents
- Copy of resumés of all principals
- Copies of letters of intent from suppliers, etc.

Note: Include all assumptions upon which projections were based.

Appendices

Include details and studies used in your business plan, for example:

- Brochures and advertising materials
- Industry studies
- Magazine or other articles
- Detailed lists of equipment owned or to be purchased
- Letters of support from future suppliers and customers
- Any other materials needed to support the assumptions in this plan
- Market research studies
- List of assets available as collateral for a loan

"Risk comes from not knowing what you're doing."
Warren Buffet

10

Accounting

Your ultimate goal is to run a profitable business. You can only do this if you stay in touch with where your money is coming from, and, just as importantly, where your money is going.

Accounting is the system that keeps track of data, provides reports, payroll, and tax status. Recording your transactions and information is called bookkeeping, and it must be done regularly. Having record keeping systems in place before you launch your business is highly advised.

Many of your business expenses can be deducted from your taxes. Therefore, good record keeping can save you money and will definitely be to your advantage if you were ever to be audited by the IRS.

Accounting is about money in and money out, but it is also about your databases of customers, vendors, and employees. Capturing and maintaining information on these people will help you keep track of how you are doing and how to grow your business in the future.

The best way to make accounting successful is to establish an accounting system.

Do I Need a CPA?

One question that will come up immediately is whether or not you need a *Certified Public Accountant* (CPA). For most people, the answer is 'Yes', since a CPA can help you set up and maintain your accounting system, generate the reports you will need to manage your business, provide annual audits, and help you with your tax planning.

Some things to look for in a CPA are:

- License to practice
- Experience with your type of business
- References
- Hours of availability
- Trust
- Feeling comfortable with them

The best way to find a CPA is through referrals from other professionals such as your banker or lawyer.

Accounting Software

Software can make your bookkeeping and accounting easier and more efficient. It will allow you to type in an expense and the software system will put it where it belongs.

Accounting software has different modules dealing with different areas of accounting.

- *Accounts Receivable* — where the company enters money received
- *Accounts Payable* — where the company enters its bills and pays money it owes
- General Ledger — the company's "books"

- Billing — where the company produces invoices to clients/customers
- Stock/Inventory — where the company keeps control of its inventory
- Purchase Order — where the company orders inventory
- Sales Order — where the company records customer orders (the supply of inventory to customers)

Additional modules offered by some software might include:

- Debt Collection — where the company tracks attempts to collect overdue bills
- Electronic Payment Processing
- Expense — where employee and business-related expenses are entered
- Payroll — where the company tracks salary, wages, and related taxes
- Reports — where the company prints out data
- Timesheet — where professionals record time worked so that it can be billed to clients
- Purchase Requisition — where requests for purchase orders are made, approved and tracked

Inexpensive applications software is now available that can perform most general business accounting functions. Some business accounting software is designed for specific business types. Though more expensive, it will include features that are specific to that industry.

Every small business needs to know where the money went - and is going. Let's look at a few top accounting programs to help you do just that.

Note: See Part One, Chapter Four: Software, 'Accounting Software' section for a full review of the most popular accounting software currently available.

Setting Up an Accounting System

There are two ways you can set up your accounting system: *cash basis* or *accrual basis*. You have a cash basis if sales are paid without billing and you purchase items without billing. If you bill or are billed for goods and services, the accrual basis may work best for you. Accountants usually recommend the accrual basis to get a better picture of how your business is doing.

Consult an accountant to determine the best method for setting up your accounting system.

Opening Your Business Bank Account

Opening a business bank account is an important step for creating a business identity as the IRS requires you to keep your personal funds and business funds completely separate. When considering a bank, look at the following:

- **Online facilities**, such as online banking, a Merchant ID, credit card processing facilities etc.

- **A bank that is close to your place of business**. If you also have a brick-and-mortar office or retail outlet, this will make depositing and withdrawing funds easier.

- **The charges that apply for various services**. Services may incur fees if you drop below a set minimum balance, if you write more than a certain number of checks, or if you go beyond a certain number of teller visits. Consider all of these fees carefully – it really can add up.

- **Size**. Smaller, local banks take more time out to help new businesses in their community. Larger, national banks have more services. Look at both kinds of banks to determine your needs and how their services fit your needs.

The recent economic crisis has reminded us all of the importance of banks regarding the long term safety of your money. Play safe with your money; choose a bank with a good reputation and a good rating for future safety.

If you are considering a totally Internet-based operation and want to work from a laptop on a beach, or if you want to run your own offshore company, then choose an offshore bank that has worldwide coverage. For example, HSBC has branches worldwide from which you can deposit or withdraw your company's cash.

"Risk comes from not knowing what you're doing."
Warren Buffet

11

Taxes and Your Business

As a small business, there are several different taxes you will need to be aware of. Failure to pay and collect appropriate taxes can cause a lot of trouble with the IRS.

Employment Taxes

If you have employees, you will have to pay employment taxes – taxes that you withhold from your employees' wages to pay local, state, and federal taxes.

The type of state and local taxes will vary depending on your city and state, Federal taxes include the following:

- *Federal income tax withholding*: Withholding acts as a prepayment of tax an employee will owe at the end of the year. A refund is issued if the withholding was greater than the tax owed. To figure how much to withhold from each wage payment, use the employee's Form W-4 and the methods described in IRS Publication 15, Employers Tax Guide (www.irs.gov/publications/p15/index.html).

- *Social Security and Medicare Taxes*: These taxes are used to pay for benefits received under the *Federal Insurance Contributions Act* (FICA). The social security portion pays for old-age, survivors, and disability insurance and Medicare pays for the hospital insurance portion of FICA. You withhold ½ of these taxes from your employees' income and then you must pay a matching amount.

- *Federal Unemployment Tax* (FUTA): This pays for unemployment compensation to workers who lose their jobs. This tax is paid separately from the other Federal taxes. It is paid directly by the employer.

The easiest way to deposit these taxes is through the U.S. Department of Treasury's free tax payment system, *Electronic Federal Tax Payment System* (EFTPS). When using this system, you can pay your federal taxes via the Internet or phone 24/7. Visit http://www.irs.gov/efile/article/0,,id=98005,00.html for more information or to enroll.

PLATE 39: WWW.SSA.GOV

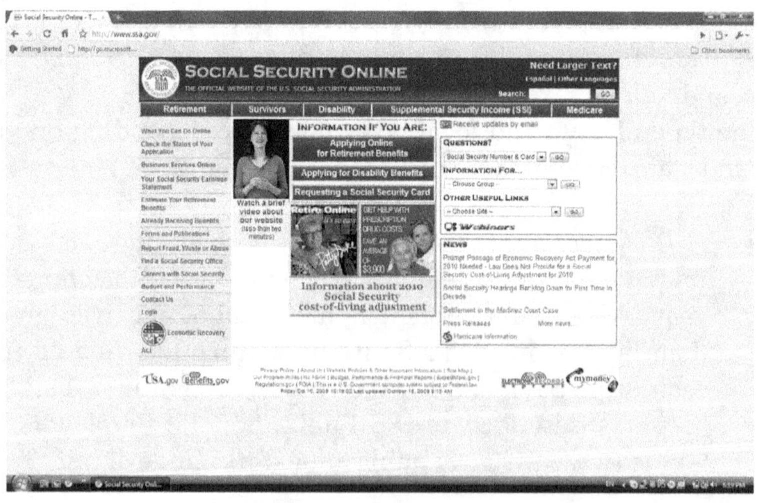

Finally, at the end of the year, you must complete *Form W-2, Wage and Tax Statement* to report all monies paid to your employees, as well as taxes withheld. A copy of the form is given to the employee and to the Social Security Administration. You can prepare these W-2s at the SSA's website (http://www.ssa.gov/bso/bsowelcome.htm).

Forms for Reporting Taxes

Withholding, Social Security and Medicare:

- Form 941, Employer's Quarterly Federal Tax Return
- Form 943, Employer's Annual Federal Tax Return for Agriculture Employees (For use by farm employers)
- Form 944, Employer's Annual Federal Tax Return

Unemployment:

Form 940, Employer's Annual Federal Unemployment (FUTA) Tax Return

---

Self-Employment Tax

Self-Employment Tax (SE Tax) is a Social Security and Medicare tax used for those that work for themselves. You determine your SE tax using the IRS Schedule SE (Form 1040). You can deduct half of your SE tax when determining your adjusted gross income, but you cannot deduct your Social Security or Medicare taxes. The self-employment tax rate in 2009 is 15.3%: 12.4% for social security and 2.9% for Medicare. The Schedule SE for the current year will always give you the up-to-date rate for that year.

To pay SE tax, you must have a *Social Security Number* (SSN) or an *Individual Taxpayer Identification Number* (ITIN). You can apply for a SSN by using Form SS-5, Application for a Social Security Card. Call (800) 772-1213 for any questions. If you are not eligible for a SSN, you can get an ITIN by filing Form W-7, Application for IRS Individual Taxpayer Identification Number.

To pay the SE tax, you must be self-employed. Here are the IRS standards to determine if you are self-employed and, therefore, must pay the tax:

- You carry on a trade or business as a sole proprietor or an independent contractor.
- You are a member of a partnership that carries on a trade or business.
- You are otherwise in business for yourself.

To be considered self-employed, you must be using your business to make a profit. Even if your business does not make a profit, as long as your activities are in place to do so, then you are self-employed. Your business activities can be full or part-time to qualify.

C Corporation and S Corporation Taxes

C Corporation taxes are taxes based on profits and losses and taxed directly to the company. The formula for determining the tax is complicated and should be calculated by a CPA to avoid IRS penalties.

S corporation taxes are taxes based on profits and losses but are reflected on the owners' personal income tax returns. Once again, this is a difficult tax to calculate and using a CPA is recommended.

Sales Taxes

A sales tax is charged at the point of purchase for certain goods and services. If you have a brick and mortar store, sales tax is easy to determine. You simply charge your customers the sales tax required by your jurisdiction. If you have your store in Ogden, Utah, for example, you will pay the appropriate taxes for that area. These taxes vary from jurisdiction to jurisdiction.

PLATE 40: WWW.BUSINESS.GOV/GUIDES/TAXES/STATE.HTML

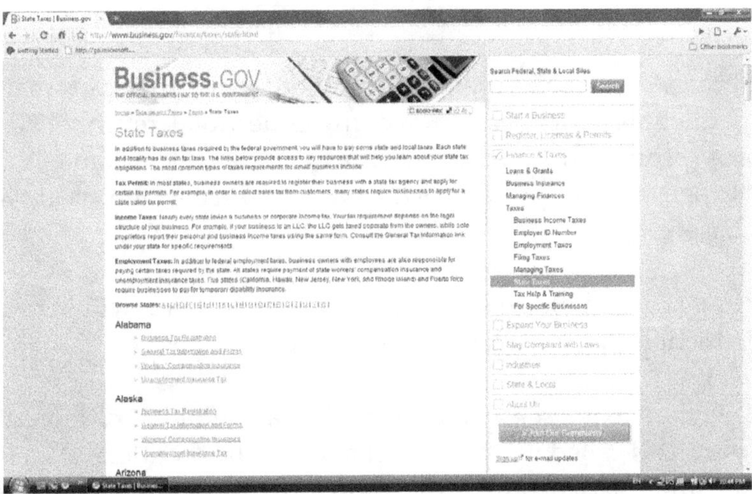

But how do sales taxes work online? If your business has a physical presence in a state, such as a store, office, or warehouse, then you are required to collect the appropriate state and local taxes for items sold. This presence is called a *nexus*. If you do not have a nexus in a state, you do not have to collect sales tax. Each state defines a nexus differently, so you should contact your state's revenue agency to determine if you will need to collect sales taxes. You can find your state's agency by going to http://www.business.gov/guides/taxes/state.html.

On the other hand, states cannot require mail-order businesses and online retailers to collect sales tax unless they have a physical presence in the state. This means that if your business is in Ogden, Utah, you will have to charge the correct taxes for your state, but those outside of Utah will not be required to pay sales tax.

Note: If you have business registered offshore with an offshore bank account then you may not be eligible to pay sales tax.

Tax Deductions

What can I deduct as expenses for my business? Expenses that are tax deductible reduce your gross revenue (total revenue) to net income (profit). This, in turn, reduces your taxable income. A cost, or "expense", is typically written off during the year it is purchased.

Tip: A good rule of thumb is that a cost or expense will generally be deductible if it has a legitimate business purpose.

When an expense, such as a car, has a useful life of more than one year, it is called a capital asset and will be "written off" a little bit at a time; based on its useful life. This is called depreciation. The IRS determines the useful life of capital assets. Be aware that expenses such as pencils or other materials that are consumed are never considered a capital asset, even if they are bought in December and not used until March. The cost is to be deducted in the year purchased, not the year used.

To learn more about depreciation, you can go to the IRS website:
http://www.irs.gov/publications/p946/ch01.html#d0e896

Tip: Depreciation of assets does not include small items even if they have a useful life. For example, something like a 3-hole punch is an insignificant purchase and can be considered a simple deduction. Unless a purchase is of approximately $300 or more, never consider it to be a capital asset.

When you have a partnership, S Corporation, or LLC, you may want to use the *Section 179* tax tool. This allows your business to *expense* up to $112,000 of certain equipment and capital assets in the year of purchase instead of having to depreciate them over time. Section 179 can be used to reinvest in the business and avoid income taxes.

Finally, you need to look at *startup expenses*. These expenses can include:

- Cost of travel
- Trade shows
- Educational or training seminars
- Accounting and legal fees
- Consulting fees
- Building costs
- Supplies or materials needed to get your business started (not inventory or raw materials)
- Fees paid to obtain licenses
- Accounting or legal fees for formation of the entity

You will be able to expense up to $5,000 for each startup cost and up to $5,000 for organizational costs. Costs over $5,000 must be written off over 15 years. For example, if you attend seminars totaling $7,500 prior to starting your business, you will be able to deduct $5,000 as a startup expense and then will have to write off the remaining $2,500 over the next 15 years.

However, if you were to go to the same show after you open your business, this would be considered a regular business expense and can be completely written off in that year.

Determining which way is best for you regarding tax, is best determined by a CPA or other tax professional.

HOME OFFICE DEDUCTIONS

If you use a portion of your home for business purposes on a *"regular and exclusive" basis*, you may be able to take a *home office* deduction.

By the IRS definition, *exclusive* means you have dedicated a specific area of your home to conduct your business or trade or to meet with clients or customers. When the agency says regular, it means the area is used regularly for your business. Incidental or occasional business use is not regular use. You do not meet the requirements of exclusive business use if the area in question is used for both business and personal purposes.

Expenses you may be able to deduct for business use of the home include:

- A portion of your home's real estate taxes
- Mortgage interest or rent
- Utilities
- Insurance
- Depreciation
- Painting and repairs

(To find out what qualifies as a deductible business expense, go to http://www.irs.gov/smallbiz. Then search for "business expenses.")

Your deductions in these expense categories are determined by the percentage of your home that is used to conduct your small business. Computing the business percentage is easy; divide the area used for your business by the total area of the home.

For example, if you have a 2000 square foot home and use 250 square feet for your business, the business percentage would be:

$$250 / 2000 = .125 \times 100 = 12.5 \text{ percent}$$

To determine your home office deduction, multiply the percentage of your home that is used for business by your allowable indirect household expenses, like electricity and gas. Then you add your direct expenses. In the example above, 12.5 percent of your indirect expenses are deductible.

To fully understand the IRS rules in this area, you need to read *Publication 587* "Business Use of Your Home." The publication is available at http://www.irs.gov or by calling 800-829-3676.

If you claim a home office deduction, you should keep meticulous records of all your expenses and be prepared to back them up if you are asked to by the IRS. As with most tax matters, it is a good idea to check with a CPA or tax attorney if you have any questions.

"Risk comes from not knowing what you're doing."
Warren Buffet

12

Your Small Business Insurance Needs

There are many different types of business insurance that you should be aware of. Let's look at the following five types:

- Property Insurance
- Casualty Insurance
- Liability Insurance
- Commercial Auto Insurance
- Worker's Compensation Insurance

Property Insurance

Property insurance insures against loss or damage to the location of the business and its contents. Property insurance can be for a specific risk (*single peril*) such as fire, or tornado specifically, or for a broader range of risks (*broad form*). The more risks your policy covers, the higher the premium will be.

Property insurance for small business is typically included in a package of needed insurances known as a *business owner's policy*. This will typically be the best value for your money as long as you qualify.

Most property insurance policies can be modified by adding coverage (*endorsements*), subtracting coverage (*exclusions*), and specifying locations of coverage (*schedules*).

Property insurance can pay damages or loss based on one of two ways:

- **Actual Cash Value (ACV)** – *Actual Cash Value* means that your loss or damage is valued using the actual cash value of the lost property (i.e. the amount in cash that you paid for it).

- **Replacement Value** – *Replacement Value* means that you are reimbursed the amount necessary to replace the lost equipment (i.e. the amount in cash that you will need to replace the property). Replacement value coverage typically carries higher premiums.

Casualty Insurance

Many insurance packages will put casualty and property insurance together and these packages often offer the best deal. Nonetheless, it is good to know what *casualty insurance* includes.

Casualty insurance insures against loss or damage to the business itself due to business interruption or other indirect losses. For instance, if you have an office complex on the top floor of a high rise and there is damage to the first floor that will interrupt your business operations, casualty, not property, insurance will pay for your losses.

Types of casualty insurance that are typically excluded from basic packages and must be bought separately include:

- Terrorism
- Flood
- Political Risk
- Cyber Liability
- Identity Theft
- Employee Theft
- Cyber Fraud, etc.

Liability Insurance

Liability Insurance insures against negligence of your business or employees. In other words, it protects your business when it is sued for neglect. Once again, for small businesses, liability insurance is often included in the business owner's package. You can also get liability insurance through a general liability policy that is separate from the package.

You can have a liability policy that is a *claims made policy* or an *occurrence policy*. A claims made policy means that the company that currently insures your business will pay the claim regarding something that happened long ago, even if they were not the insurer at that time. For instance, if you are a builder and a defect is determined 10 years after the construction is finished, your current insurance company will be your insurer.

The occurrence policy means that the insurance company that insured you at the time the problem occurred will handle the claim. In the same example, the builder would be covered instead by the insurance company that insured him 10 years ago.

What is covered and not covered often depends upon the laws of your state. However, all of the following are **not** covered:

- Injury to a worker
- Damage or loss caused by a company vehicle
- Damage to business property
- Pollution

Commercial Auto

Your personal auto insurance does not cover vehicles used by your business. Therefore, you will need *commercial auto coverage*. A commercial auto policy provides coverage to repair or replace a vehicle damaged in an accident and it will pay the claims of any third-party injured in the accident.

You can purchase *"non-owned auto" coverage* as well. This coverage will provide coverage to your business when employees use their personal vehicles for business purposes or if your business uses any car it does not own.

Worker's Compensation

You will need to insure your employees against on-the-job injuries with *worker's compensation.* Every state has different rules concerning worker's compensation but most states have some form of coverage.

Worker's compensation keeps an employee from suing your company for on-the-job injuries. For this protection, you must provide for their medical bills and coverage. By law, you will be required to participate in workers' compensation unless you are a self-employed sole trader.

The initial insurance premiums will be based on the typical claims that are likely to occur in your industry. Industries with less chance of injury, such as office worker, have lower premiums than those, such as construction, that have higher risks.

After a period of time set by your state, your rates will be based on your actual claims. You will have higher premiums for higher than average claims and lower premiums for lower than average claims.

Different States Have Different Worker's Compensation Laws

North Dakota, Ohio, Washington, West Virginia, and Wyoming:

The state sets rates and operates a state-administered fund of workers compensation insurance.

California, Delaware, D.C., Indiana, Massachusetts, Michigan, Minnesota, New Jersey, New York, North Carolina, Wisconsin:

These states allow private insurers to provide workers compensation, subject to ratings and administration developed by that particular state.

Texas:

Allows some employers to have no insurance.

All other states not listed above:

Allow private insurance and are rated by the National Council on Compensation Insurance (NCCI). These states are referred to as "NCCI" states.

Choosing an Insurance Company

Getting the correct, relevant and sufficient insurance at the optimum cost is an important cost factor for any business; insufficient cover or paying too much for your cover is bad business.

PLATE 41: WWW.NAIC.ORG/STATE_WEB_MAP.HTM

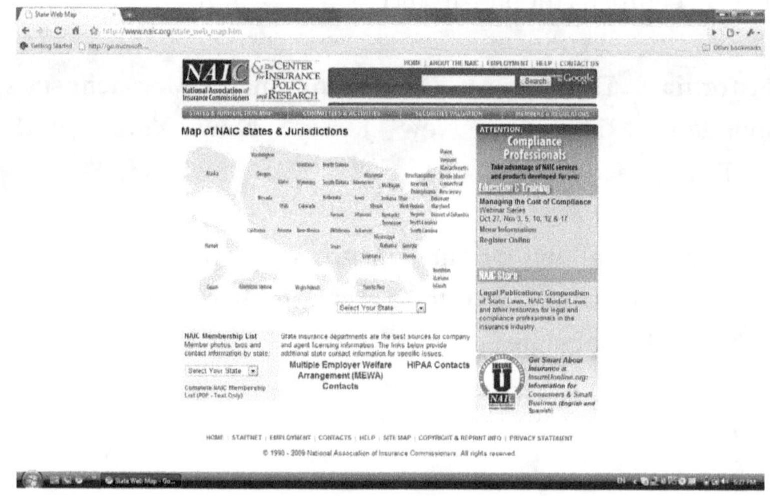

Here are some things to consider in choosing an insurance company for your business insurance:

- Price: The cost of coverage can vary greatly from one insurer to the next without any difference in coverage

- Stability: Companies are rated for their stability by various rating services such as A.M. Best, or Standard & Poor. Consider companies with a Best's Rating of B+ or better

- Excellent Service

- Physical Location: Company with a physical location in your state and registered to sell insurance in your state. You can determine this by going to your state insurance department: http://www.naic.org/state_web_map.htm

- Choice of Counsel: Allows you to pick your own attorney to defend you in case of a lawsuit

"Risk comes from not knowing what you're doing."
Warren Buffet

13

Choosing Your Business Setting

You have many different options when choosing where your business will be located. Let's look at a few of the most common.

Working from a Home Office

Many people view a home office as a wonderful idea and an easy option. And it can be. However, it can also be frustrating. The difference between wonderful and frustrating is proper planning. Here are some guidelines to help you:

- You will need to have a special place set aside for your office. It can be a den, office, spare bedroom, unused dining room, garage, or any appropriate space. It is preferable that this space has a door that will separate your workspace from your living space.

- Keep your workspace dedicated to work. This means keeping distractions to a minimum. Such distractions can be the TV, computer games, or even family members.

- If you have small children at home, you will want to work when a caregiver is available.

- Having small children in your home office is very distracting, and should be avoided.

- Make your workspace comfortable.

- Make your workspace organized, with filing cabinets, folders, labels, in-boxes, etc.

- Create a schedule that best suits you. Be sure to schedule breaks, lunch, and other needs.

- Determine at what time work is over for the day. Becoming a workaholic is very typical among those that work at home. Once your day is over, close the door to the office and don't go back in. Once again, this is setting the office boundaries. It works both ways.

- Don't become isolated. Working from home can keep you insulated from others; maintain a business and social network.

- You will not want to use your home address as your business address. You can either use a Post Office Box, a 'virtual' office address, or a *Commercial Mail Receiving Agency (CMRA)* mailbox service that gives you a corporate-sounding address and a suite number. Either way, you are going to have to go pick up your mail. Also, keep in mind that many companies, such as UPS, will not deliver a package to a PO Box. With a CMRA you can receive packages, have 24-hour access, and request notification when a package has arrived.

Working from a Virtual Company

A company that does not have a physical location is called a *virtual company*. Rather, it is more like a collection of individuals that each work from their home offices. You would have a home office, as would all of your employees, but your company would have a single business address.

In addition to standard office equipment, a computer, and an Internet connection, you may also need specific software to coordinate scheduling, access central files, maintain a contact manager, and meet in chat rooms etc.

Virtual Company Software

There are online management services that provide these types of services on the Internet for access with your browser. These are fairly simple to use. They offer many features to promote coordination of information between members of a team, client interactions, or simply communication and share files with co-workers. They typically charge a small monthly fee per user, or a larger flat rate for unlimited users.

Some of these management services include free limited versions. Below are some of these services available on the Internet:

VISTO

Visto Mobile Enterprise Edition is a server-based software that is installed inside the corporate firewall and integrates with either Microsoft Exchange or IBM Lotus Domino to provide mobile workers with instant and secure access to corporate data, all from their mobile phone. Price varies greatly among different phone providers and with different functionality.

VIRTUAL OFFICE

AfterOffice's Virtual Office is an Enterprise Portal service targeted at the SME business community worldwide, offering a wide and comprehensive range of integrated scheduling, business communication and collaborations, and information management applications. It provides a secure space on the web where you and your team can easily access and share documents, calendars, and conduct online meeting and discussion anywhere, anytime, from any web-enabled devices. $180 per year.

PLATE 42: VIRTUAL OFFICES WEBSITE

OFFICECLIP

OfficeClip Premium Suite provides a complete business management solution. It includes Timesheet and Expense Tracking, Contact Manager for your Marketing and Sales Team, Issue Tracker for tracking development and related issues and Collaboration Suite (web calendar, web document sharing, etc). OfficeClip Premium Suite can be purchased for $80 per user.

NOODLE

Noodle provides a mixture of serious business application and people-centric social-based tools. It has an easy-to-use interface and offers flexible deployment options, such as local server installs or software. Noodle costs between $39-$125 per employee.

PLATE 43: NOODLE VIRTUAL OFFICES SOFTWARE

Your software needs will vary greatly depending on the type of work you are doing. Check with similar businesses or your industry association to find out what programs are preferred by your peers.

Virtual Office Policies

If you have employees in several different locations, having a set of office guidelines will help your workflow. You may want to consider:

- Procedures for logging in to the system will help you manage the security of your system.

- Procedures for accessibility during business hours will help the communication between one another.

- Procedures for forwarding calls or emails if an employee is unavailable will help keep the business flowing smoothly.

- Procedures for client interactions will keep your business on a professional level. This includes email protocols, traditional correspondence protocols, and any other interactions typical in your business.

Legal Ramifications of a Home or Virtual Office

When you have a traditional home office or a home office as part of a network of offices, you need to consider the legalities. You need to look at:

ZONING

Is your home in an area zoned for business? What type of business can you operate from your home? Check out your local zoning ordinances to make sure you don't have to get any special permits or licensing, or have any restrictions on what you can do from your home.

TAX ISSUES

If you want to claim a home office, the IRS has specific requirements to follow. So, if you're working from your dining room table, then you probably can't take that home office deduction. Contact your tax accountant or attorney to find out the laws as they pertain to your situation.

Thousands of people now work from home or a virtual office. Through good planning, communication, and outside technical support when needed, your home or virtual office can be an enjoyable and successful option.

Renting Space

Due to the size or needs of your business, you may decide to rent office and/or warehouse space rather than have a home or virtual office. Although the overhead is higher, the advantages may outweigh the cost concerns.

HOW MUCH SPACE WILL YOU NEED?

When deciding what purposes you need your office space to fill, think about your expected everyday activities. For instance:

- Will clients be visiting your office space? If so, you may want a reception area, good parking, and perhaps a conference area.

- Will you have employee meetings? If so, you may want meeting rooms that have computer hook ups and other meeting options such as white boards, overhead projection systems, etc.

- Will any of your employees work from both home and office? If so, you may want central workstations where anyone can plug in while in the office.

- Will you be working as a team on different projects or to create different concepts? If so, you may want areas separate from employees' offices where several employees can discuss and brainstorm without disturbing others.

- Will employees need to use the phone or be performing tasks that require quiet or privacy? If so, you may want to have private offices for these employees.

- Will your employees need a break room? If so, you may want a kitchen space.

- Will your business need a loading and shipping dock area? If so, you will have to find space that allows for this. Also, consider future products that you are not currently offering but plan to offer later when making this determination.

Once you know what you will use the space for, you will need to determine how large the space needs to be. According to OfficeFinder.com, in typical office scenarios, you can estimate 175-250 square feet per employee. However, if you know that you'll need a couple of large executive offices, then you need to estimate more square footage for those. Typical executive offices range from 150-400 square feet while administrative spaces range from 60-110 square feet.

Other areas include the meeting room space and the reception area. Typical allowances for a meeting room are 25 to 30 square feet per individual using the room. Reception spaces need to be 200 square feet if you typically have 3 to 5 people arriving at a time and 300 square feet for groups of 6 to 9.

PLATE 44: WWW.OFFICEFINDER.COM

You should compare the benefits of leasing versus buying your property from a cash standpoint, as well as the more obvious needs standpoint, such as long term space requirements and expansion possibilities. While there are benefits to both options, for startups there appear to be more benefits to leasing than buying. Cash flow is, of course, an issue and buying takes a larger portion of your hard-earned cash up front.

LEASE ISSUES TO BE AWARE OF

Many leases have something called an *Escalation Clause*. This is an annual increase built into your lease from day one. The landlord accounts for inflation, market value increases, etc. These increases can be fixed or based on a percentage of the *consumer price index*. In most cases, these are negotiable.

Be sure to read the fine print. If you don't, you may find that what you hoped to do can't be done. Check for things such as:

- Business hour limitations

- Alteration limitations
- Lease renewal restrictions
- Common area maintenance
- Administration charges
- After-hours utility costs

The most important thing to remember is that the lease is written for the benefit of the landlord, not for you. Therefore, it is important that you read everything and have your attorney read it as well.

14

How to Staff Your Office

Even if you know that you need the extra help, you'll still need to consider whether you can afford to hire a new full-time employee. Remember, 'Overheads work on two legs!' In other words, hiring an employee means salary, benefits, taxes, and worker's compensation. Staff is likely to be your most expensive cost, so choose well and don't employ more than you absolutely have to.

Once you have determined how much an employee will cost, you will need to estimate how much money that employee will make in the first year. If the employee is a sales person, then you should determine how many products you believe he or she can sell in that time. If the employee performs other functions, you may want to ask yourself these questions:

- Will you have more time to market your services and expand your business?

- Will you be able to produce more products or serve more clients?

- Will you be able to give your customers a more efficient service or quicker delivery?

If you answer 'yes' to these questions, try to estimate the amount of extra business that would be created due to these factors.

If you're fairly sure that the extra business would amount to more than the minimum salary of the employee, then you are in a good position to hire someone. If not, you may want to look at alternatives:

- Part-time Employees
- Temporary Help
- Independent Contractors
- Virtual Assistant

Part-Time Employees

A part-time employee costs less because they work less hours and often do not have the same benefits such as health care that full time employees have. Additionally, their hours are typically more flexible to fit around the times you most need them.

Temporary Help

A temporary worker can help you fill in for full time employees on vacation, sick leave, or a leave of absence. They can also be hired during particularly busy times of the year such as Christmas. Temporary help is often recruited through a temp agency. These agencies send you workers that have the qualifications you specify.

Not all business situations lend themselves to using temporary workers. For example, if the job you need to have done requires high skills or specialized skills, you may not be able to find what you need.

Independent Contractors

An *independent contractor* is particularly useful when you need a specific skill or technical knowledge for a special project that's expected to last a relatively short length of time. Independent contractors work for themselves — they are treated as if they are running their own business.

Thus, you are not the employer of an independent contractor. Because of this you will not have to pay their income, social security, and Medicare taxes and they are typically not protected by worker's compensation. Independent contractors are usually paid based on their results rather than by a standard time clock.

Here are some things you can do to help ensure that you or those who work for you qualify for independent contractor status:

- Avoid setting a regular pattern of daily or weekly hours. An independent contractor should have the opportunity to select when and where he or she will work.

- Allow contractors to supply their own tools, supplies, and equipment wherever possible in the performance of the services required.

- Use contractors who normally advertise their services in some manner.

- Allow contractors to hire their own assistants, if necessary.

- Compensate independent contractors on a per-job basis rather than by hour or by week.

- Always ask for an invoice or statement before paying for any work that has been performed.

- Make checks payable to a company rather than to an individual.

- Do not directly reimburse contractors for any expenses they might have, for gasoline, meals, etc. Such expenses should stand as part of the contractor's set fees.

- Have a written contract to show the independent contractor relationship.

Virtual Assistant

With a virtual office, you may want to consider a Virtual Assistant (VA). A VA is a secretary that has their own virtual office. They can be hired on an as-needed basis, or for an agreed amount each day, week, or month.

The benefit of using a VA is that you only pay for the time worked and not the time waiting for a phone to ring as with traditional secretaries. In addition to flexible hours and reduced costs, VAs offer a wide range of skills. Some offer basic data entry while others can provide accounting or even web design.

When hiring a VA, be sure to see samples of their work and speak to the people the VA uses as references. When you speak to the references you will want to know more than the quality of their work. You will also want to know about their speed and how well they communicated.

Independent Contractor or Employee?

The IRS has a 20-factor test that it uses to determine whether an employee is an independent contractor or an employee. Generally speaking, if the worker would be considered an employee under at least 10 of the factors, you should treat him or her as an employee. If in doubt, look at IRS Form SS-8 (www.irs.gov/pub/irs-pdf/fss8.pdf), which is the form used by the IRS to determine individual status for purposes of income and employment taxes.

"Risk comes from not knowing what you're doing."
Warren Buffet

15

Forming an Offshore Company

Most people have heard that offshore companies are tax havens, but few know exactly what the benefits of an *offshore company* can be. Let's look briefly at the different types of offshore companies.

Trading Company

With the ease of communication and the growth of the Internet, you can now attract business customers from all over the world, from every time zone. Additionally, if you choose to create a business in another country, you can find significant tax benefits.

One way to do this is to create an incorporated company as part of a trading group. This means that the offshore company will either purchase or resell goods between other group members. This essentially means that you can earn and deposit your profits in a country with a low-tax or no-tax jurisdiction.

Some of the lowest jurisdictions in terms of taxes are:

- Cyprus
- Ireland
- Isle of Man
- Panama
- The BVI
- Bahamas

Professional Services Company

If you provide professional services, you may want to consider an offshore *professional services company* for two reasons: asset protection and tax planning.

Such services include those provided by lawyers, doctors, designers, consultants, and entertainers.

The tax benefits come from acquiring clients outside of the country of residence, allowing personal income to be tax free in the offshore jurisdiction. If the company then reinvests money in that jurisdiction, money earned would also be free of tax.

The key is to be sure that your company does not get classified as a resident company in your own country or it will fall within your country's tax code.

Offshore Property Company

Another way to take advantage of having an offshore company is to invest in offshore property. The advantages of investing offshore are that:

- You can avoid inheritance taxes, and
- Allow you to sell shares rather than the property itself

You simply obtain funds, typically through a mortgage, and then purchase property in the name of your company. Whatever you loaned to your company via the mortgage, will be free from taxes.

Investment Company

If you have an offshore company, you can invest in any part of the world. Although some taxes will still need to be paid, many can be avoided. One of the biggest taxes you can avoid will be the capital gains tax.

Best Places for Offshore Companies (based on the tax rate)

Country	Corporate tax rate %
Bermuda	0
Cayman Islands	0
Channel Islands	0-20
Isle of Man	0
Cyprus	10
Barbados	1
Vanuatu	0
Bahamas	0
British Virgin Islands	0
Nevis	0
Anguilla	0
Ireland	12.5
Gibraltar	0
Panama	0

Setting up an Offshore Company

Setting up an offshore company should be done by someone who specializes in such matters. These are usually *incorporation agents*. However, here are a few things you need to know about the set up:

- Choose the country for your company
- Determine the type of entity you wish to use for your company
- Choose your company's name
- Draft the articles of association
- Determine the method of funding your company
- What method you will use to issue shares
- Determine the directors of your company

Typically, setting up an offshore company, depending upon the country, takes between 1 week and 1 month.

Offshore Bank Accounting Tips

It is often advisable for foreign *domiciliaries* to have at least three overseas bank accounts:

- The first account for existing capital
- The second account to deposit the proceeds of any asset disposals
- The third account to contain the interest from the first two accounts, along with any other foreign source income

Note: The aim is to segregate your foreign income or gains.

If you want to bring money into the country you should first remit funds from the first account. This can usually be done free of tax. If further funds are required, then withdrawals can be made from the second account, which could effectively subject the withdrawals to capital gains tax. Finally, withdrawals from the third account would be subject to income tax.

If you're going for an offshore structure Panama is probably one of the best options. A Panama trust or foundation, holding a company with a Panamanian bank account (e.g. Banco General HSBC Panama, Banco National) is a sound choice.

To take full advantage of moving your business offshore, you should do the following:

- Register your company offshore (e.g. Costa Rica)
- Have your website hosted offshore (e.g. Hong Kong)
- Open a bank account offshore (e.g. Panama)

The advantage of setting up your business this way is that it allows you to access all profits outside the USA (or whichever country you reside in) tax free.

Mobile and Remote Offices

An offshore bank account and a website hosted outside your country of residence allows you to administer your website from anywhere in the world and withdraw your company's money from an ATM anywhere on the face of the earth… tax free!

Thousands of people are now running online businesses from a laptop on a beach. Due to new technology, there is now no logistical reason why you shouldn't run your entire commercial operations from a smart phone while lying in a hammock! If you want to know more, just let me know.

Summary

Although you may wonder if being online is truly necessary, the answer is that it most definitely is. Being online means:

1. Your business is open to everyone all the time. No matter what time of day or night, no matter what the day of the week, no matter where your customers live, you have the opportunity to meet their needs.

2. No matter what you sell, it can be updated immediately, anytime and there is no need to reprint expensive promotional materials.

3. You can easily reach out to new markets. On the Internet, you aren't that local little business anymore.

4. Your customer service will improve because you can answer questions on your website before they are even asked.

5. Your website provides you with a professional image. This will instill confidence in your clients that you are able to do for them what needs to be done.

6. Selling in cyberspace is cheaper than selling in a "brick-n-mortar" business with rent, electric bills, and other costs. And even if you have a "brick-n-mortar" business, you can supplement your business with an extra volume of sales.

7. If you have a service-oriented business, you can promote your business, offering potential clients a choice among your competitors. Millions of users are referring to the web

and are using companies' websites to make major decisions when they need a specialized service.

8. You can gather information about your customers using forms and surveys so that you can offer further products or services.

9. If you offer downloadable products, you can fulfill the modern need of instant gratification. You can even offer free samples or trials to download.

10. Finally, e-commerce is the future; online retail sales rose 17% by the beginning of 2009 to $204 billion. You certainly want to be part of this incredible sales opportunity by creating an e-commerce business or giving your old business e-commerce capabilities.

Checklist

1. What are you going to sell? *
2. Choose your company name
3. Register your company name
4. Choose your domain name
5. Register your domain name
6. Determine where your office will be located
7. Consider offshore options
8. Choose a legal entity
9. Get an Employer Identification Number (EIN)
10. Create a detailed business plan
11. Find a CPA
12. Acquire accounting software
13. Set up an accounting system
14. Open a business bank account
15. Learn about tax payments
16. Keep records for tax deductions
17. Purchase insurance
18. Determine how to staff your office
19. Get a credit card processing facility
20. Now you're ready to make $ERIOUS MONEY Online!

* The book, 'Fortune Cookie' explains in detail how to go about deciding on the perfect product or service for you to sell online.

Included in the purchase of this book is the opportunity to download an example business plan of a digital camera business (digital cameras are an excellent example of a product that sells very well online).

Go to www.riskeliminator.com/free_downloads and use the word **precursor** as the password.

The unique selling proposition of this particular business is that it specializes in underwater or sports cameras.

To help ensure that your online business is a successful one, it is vitally important to target a niche. Therefore, please use this business plan as a guide to write your own plan about a target niche you have identified. To help you identify an online niche, visit www.riskeliminator.com.

Good Luck!

Dr. Richard G. Lewis FCIM
www.riskeliminator.com

"Risk comes from not knowing what you're doing."
Warren Buffet

Glossary

12-month Profit and Loss Projection
Acts as a guide to help you forecast your company's sales and expenses over a 12-month period of time.

Accounting
The classifying, summarizing and interpreting in a significant manner and in terms of money, transactions and events of a financial character.

Accounts Payable
Bills and money owed.

Accounts Receivable
Money received.

Accrual Basis
An accounting method in which income and expense items are credited as they are incurred or earned.

Actual Cash Value
The value of property based on the cost of repairing or replacing it with property of the same kind and quality. Also known as 'market value'.

Anti-Virus Program
A software program designed to identify and remove a known or potential computer virus.

Asset
Anything owned by an individual or a business that has commercial or exchange value.

Balance Sheet
A financial statement that reports the assets, liabilities and equity of an entity as at a particular date.

Bitmap Image
A bitmap is a type of image file format used to store digital images. The name bitmap comes from the computer programming terminology, meaning just a map of bits, a spatially mapped array of bits.

Board of Directors
A body of elected or appointed persons who jointly oversee the activities of a company or organization.

Bookkeeping
The process of recording business transactions into the accounting records.

Botnet
A type of Remote Control Software, specifically a collection of software robots, or "bots", which run autonomously.

Break-even Analysis
The breakeven point for a product is the point where total revenue received equals the total costs associated with the sale of the product.

Broadband
Broadband Internet access, often shortened to just "broadband", is high-speed Internet access.

Broad Form
Coverage for numerous perils.

Bugs
An error, flaw, mistake, failure, or fault in a computer program that prevents it from working as intended.

Business Plan
A written document that details a proposed or existing venture. It will typically explain the vision, current status, expected needs, defined markets, and projected results of the business.

C Corporation
A standard business corporation. It is called a C corporation because it is taxed under subsection C of the IRS code.

Capital
Assets available for use in the production of further assets.

Capital Asset
All of a company's tangible property, including securities, real estate and other property.

Cash Basis
An accountancy reporting method that recognizes cash inflows or outflows when actually expended or received.

Casualty Insurance
The type of insurance concerned with the legal liability for losses caused by injury to others or damage to property of others.

Certified Public Accountant (CPA)
An accountant who has passed the necessary exams and fulfilled age and experience requirements as dictated by the state in which they work.

Claims Made Policy
A liability insurance policy under which a written claim is made during the policy period or any extended reporting period.

Commercial Auto Insurance
A standard business automobile policy that is designed to cover the liability and physical damage of motor vehicles. Liability coverage can be provided for the organization, regardless of whether a nonprofit, a staff member, volunteer or other party owns the vehicle.

Commercial Mail Receiving Agency (CMRA)
Also known as a mail drop, typically operates as a Private Mail Box Operator.

Consumer Price Index
A measure of the average price of consumer goods and services purchased by households.

Copyright
The legal right granted to an author, composer, playwright, publisher, or distributor to exclusive publication, production, sale, or distribution of a literary, musical, dramatic, or artistic work.

Corporation
A corporation is a legal entity (technically, a juristic person) which has a legal personality distinct from those of its members.

CPU (Computer Processing Unit)
The part of a computer that interprets and executes instructions.

CRT (Cathode Ray Tube)
Device whereby electrons are sprayed onto a viewing screen, under the direction of magnetic fields, to form patterns. Examples of CRTs include television screens and computer terminals.

Data
The information required by the computer to be able to operate.

Depreciation
The decline in the value of a capital asset. Depreciation represents a cost of ownership and the consumption of an asset's useful life.

Desktop Email
Programs that only allow you to check your email from your own computer or with access to your own computer.

DNS IP Address
A numerical identification that is assigned to devices participating in a computer network.

Domain Name
The unique name that identifies an Internet website.

Domain Name Registrar
Any entity that acts on behalf of a registrant regarding domain name requests or modifications.

Domiciliary
A person who legally resides in a particular place.

E-book
A book's contents that are in an electronic format.

E-commerce
The online transaction of business, featuring linked computer systems of the vendor, host, and buyer.

Electronic Federal Tax Payment System (EFTPS)
The primary method that the U.S. government uses to collect taxes.

Email
A message sent or received electronically over a computer network, as between personal computers.

Employer Identification Number (EIN)
Uniquely identifies every tax-paying entity in the United States.

Employment Taxes
Federal income tax withholding, Social Security tax, Medicare tax, and federal unemployment tax that an employer must submit on behalf of employees.

Endorsement

An agreement added to an insurance policy to change the amount of coverage offered by that policy.

Ethernet Card

An expansion board that connects a PC, or PCs, to a network.

Exclusion

A clause in a policy which specifies what is excluded from the policy's coverage.

Executive Summary

The portion of a business plan that summarizes all of the sections of the report.

Expense

An expense is an outgoing of money to another person, company or group to pay for goods or services, or for a category of costs, that can be reclaimed.

Federal Income Tax Withholding

The amount of money automatically withheld each month to be paid towards an employee's income tax contribution.

Federal Insurance Contributions Act (FICA)

A payroll deduction for Social Security required by the federal government.

Federal Unemployment Tax

Provides for payments of unemployment compensation to workers who have lost their jobs.

Financial Plan

Consists of a 12-month profit and loss projection, a four-year profit and loss projection (optional), a cash-flow projection, projected balance sheet(s) (usually between one and three years), and a break-even calculation. Together they constitute a reasonable estimate of your company's financial future.

Firewall
Any of a number of security systems and software that prevent unauthorized users from gaining access to a computer network or that monitor transfers of information to and from the network.

Focal Range
Determines a camera's angle of view. Wide angle lenses have small focal lengths, while telephoto lenses have larger corresponding focal lengths. 35mm to 70mm is what is called a "normal" focal length and comes standard with most digital cameras.

Form W-2, Wage and Tax Statement
An IRS tax form that shows wages earned and taxes withheld.

FTP (File Transfer Protocol)
Ability to transfer files from one computer to another over a network.

Gross Revenue
The total revenue in a reporting period.

GHz
A unit of frequency equal to one billion (109) hertz.

GUI (Graphical User Interface)
Graphical user interfaces are images with hotlinks that allow users to interact with electronic devices such as computers. A GUI offers graphical icons, and visual indicators, as opposed to text-based interfaces, typed command labels or text navigation to represent the information and actions available to a user.

Hard Drive
The primary computer storage device. Also called hard disk drive.

Hardware
Anything to do with the computer which is tangible.

Hertz
A unit of frequency equal to one cycle per second.

Home Office
A part of your home or other structure on your property for which you qualify to take a deduction for its business use.

HTML (Hypertext Markup Language)
The document format used on the web. Web pages are built with HTML codes embedded in the text. HTML defines a web page's layout, fonts and graphic elements.

Imaging Editor
Allows you to perform various image manipulation/editing and retouching features to refine, correct or enhance your existing image before including it in your website.

Industrial Design
The functionality and external appearance of a finished product.

Incorporation Agent
A company that helps new businesses incorporate.

Independent Contractor
A person working under a contract for the provision of services, as distinct from a contract of service, in which an employer/employee relationship exists.

Individual Taxpayer Identification Number (ITIN)
An alternative to a Social Security number, which is used for federal and state taxation purposes.

Information Security Management System (ISMS)
A set of policies concerned with information management.

In-house
Conducted within, coming from, or being within an organization or group.

Intellectual Property
A product of the intellect that has commercial value, including copyrighted property such as literary or artistic works, and ideational property, such as patents, appellations of origin, business methods, and industrial processes.

Internet Browser
A graphical tool designed to read HTML documents and access the web.

ISP (Internet Service Providers)
A company which primarily offers their customers access to the Internet.

Keylogger
Used to record every keystroke by a computer's user to allow malware to steal financial account information and passwords.

Keystroke
Every character or number typed on a keyboard.

Keyword
The basis of search engine rankings is keywords and a website's keywords; these determine the theme of a website.

LCD
A thin, flat screen or display device made up of any number of color or monochrome pixels arrayed in front of a light source or reflector.

Least-privilege Access
To give users only the access and privileges they need to complete the task at hand.

Legal Name
The name under which the business conducts its operations.

Liability Insurance
Protection for a policyholder, up to an agreed figure, for amounts payable to another individual for personal (bodily) injury or property damage.

Liability Protection
Insurance that covers people (other than the insured) and their personal property in cases of injury or damage while on the homeowner's property.

Liable
Subject to legal action.

Limited Liability Company
Business organization that offers the advantages of liability protection with the simplicity of a partnership.

Mac
A family of desktop and laptop computers from Apple and the first computer to popularize the graphical user interface (GUI).

Malware
Software designed to infiltrate or damage a computer system without the owner's informed consent.

Megapixel
A megapixel is equivalent to 1 million pixels, and is a term used not only for the number of pixels in an image, but also to express the number of image sensor elements of digital cameras or the number of display elements of digital displays. For example, a camera with an array of 2048×1536 sensor elements is commonly said to have "3.1 megapixels" (2048 × 1536 = 3,145,728).

Mission Statement
A statement that makes clear the company's purpose, principal business aims, identity, policies and values.

Modem
A device for transmitting digital data over telephone wires.

Net Income
The company's total earnings, reflecting revenues adjusted for costs of doing business, depreciation, interest, taxes and other expenses.

Network
A system of computers interconnected by telephone wires or other means in order to share information.

Nexus
A connection or link.

Non-owned Auto Coverage
Auto coverage for your employees as they drive their own vehicles or vehicles your company does not own.

Occurrence Policy
Covers claims that are reported during the policy period.

OCR (Optical Character Recognition)
Used to convert scanned text documents to editable text files.

Offshore Company
An offshore company is a company which does not conduct substantial business in its country of incorporation.

Open Source Software
Open Source Software is software for which the underlying code has been made available for users. Users are then able to read it or change it as they wish.

Operational Plan
A description of how the work will be done, the flow of work from input to end results, including the machines which will be used.

Overhead Expense
Production and nonproduction costs not readily traceable to specific jobs or processes.

Packet
A formatted block of data carried by a computer network.

Packet Sniffer
Software designed for checking packets of data transferred over the Internet.

Partnership
Type of business entity in which owners share with each other the profits or losses of the business in which all have invested.

Password
A sequence of characters that one must input to gain access to a file, application, or computer system.

Patent
Confers upon the creator of an invention the sole right to make, use, and sell that invention for a set period of time.

PC
A 'Personal Computer' (PC) is a computer built around a microprocessor for use by an individual, as in an office or at home or school.

PDF (Portable Document Format)
A universal file format that preserves the fonts, images, graphics, and layout of any source document, regardless of the application and platform used to create it.

Peripheral
An auxiliary device, such as a printer, modem, or storage system, that works in conjunction with a computer.

Personal Financial Statement
A summary of an entrepreneur's current personal financial condition.

Personal Net Worth
A person's total assets, less total liabilities.

Phishing
The act of sending an email to a user falsely claiming to be an established legitimate enterprise in an attempt to scam the user into surrendering private information that will be used for identity theft.

Primary Nameserver
The server that houses all the authoritative information regarding a website's domain and IP address.

Professional Services Company
A business that provides services rather than goods.

Projected Cash Flow
Evaluates your business income and expenses to determine earnings or losses at a future date.

Property Insurance
Insurance providing financial protection against the loss of, or damage to, real and personal property caused by a covered peril.

RAM (Random Access Memory)
A memory device used by programs to perform necessary tasks, in which information can be accessed in any order and all storage locations are equally accessible.

Regular and Exclusive Basis
A portion of your home used exclusively for business purposes on a regular basis.

Replacement Value
The full cost to repair or replace the damaged property with no deduction for depreciation, subject to policy limits and contract provisions.

Resolution
The measure of sharpness or fineness of detail that can be distinguished in an image (as on a video display, camera, scanner, printer etc.). Usually measured in the total number or density of pixels (e.g. 5000 dots per square inch).

Sales Forecast
A prediction of what sales will be achieved over a given period, anything from a week to a year.

Schedule
Specific locations of insurance coverage.

Secondary Nameserver
Ensures that the domain does not go off-line if there should happen to be a problem with the primary nameserver.

Section 179
Allows a sole proprietor, partnership or corporation to fully expense tangible property in the year it is purchased.

Server
A computer that processes requests for HTML and other documents that are components of web pages.

Social Security Number (SSN)
A number issued to people by the U.S. government for payroll deductions for old age, survivors, and disability insurance.

Self-employment Tax
Social security tax imposed on the self-employed.

Shareholder
Any holder of one or more shares in a corporation.

Shopping Cart
An Internet-based system designed to allow an online shopper to collect items and then, when the user is ready, to purchase the chosen items.

Single Peril
Insurance that covers only one specified type of risk.

SMART Goals
Acronym used to describe goal setting; specific, measurable, attainable, realistic, and time-based.

Social Security and Medicare Tax
Taxes that pay for old age, disability, death benefits, and hospital insurance. Also known as FICA taxes.

Software
Term used for the instructions or programs executed by a computer, as opposed to the physical hardware that enables the machine to follow them.

Sole Proprietorship
A business owned and managed by one person (or for tax purposes, a husband and wife).

Spam
Unsolicited email, often of a commercial nature, sent to multiple mailing lists, individuals, or newsgroups. Also known as junk email.

Spreadsheet
An accounting or bookkeeping program that displays data in rows and columns on a screen, allowing the user to capture, display, and manipulating data and make automated calculations.

SS-4 Form
Application for Employer Identification Number.

Start-up Expenses
Money invested at the start-up of a business that is paid one time and does not include monthly expenses.

Stockholder
An individual who owns one or more shares of a corporation's stock, whether common or preferred stock.

Subchapter S
A corporation that has elected to be taxed under Subchapter S of the Internal Revenue Code of 1954.

Tax Deductible
An item or expense subtracted from adjusted gross income to reduce the amount of income subject to tax.

Trademark
A name, symbol, or other device identifying a product, officially registered and legally restricted to the use of the owner or manufacturer.

Trojan Horse
A virus in which malicious or harmful code is contained inside apparently harmless programming or data.

Two-factor Authentication
Two-factor authentication is a security process in which the user provides two means of identification.

Vector Image
A vector graphic is a type of image file format used to store digital images. Vector graphics can be defined by mathematical statements and has individual properties assigned to it such as color, fill, and outline. Vector graphics are resolution independent because they can be output to the highest quality at any scale.

Virus
A piece of code that is secretly introduced into a system in order to corrupt it or destroy data. Often viruses are hidden in other programs or documents and, when opened, the virus is let loose.

Virus Signature
A unique pattern of a virus that is like a fingerprint that can be used to detect and identify specific viruses.

Web Browser
Software that interprets the markup of files in HTML, formats them into web pages, and displays them to the user in a visual, graphical format.

Web Hosting
Provides space on Internet servers for the storage of websites which can be accessed by others through the network.

Web-based Email Client
Lets you access your account from anywhere with just a browser.

Wireless
A network whose interconnections are implemented without the use of wires, such as a computer network.

Word Processing
The use of a computer and specialized software to write, edit, format, print, and save text.

Workers' Compensation
Workers' compensation is a form of insurance, which provides compensation medical care for employees that are injured in the course of employment, in exchange for mandatory relinquishment of the employee's right to sue his or her employer for negligence.

Worm
A malicious program that replicates itself until it fills all of the storage space on a drive or network.

Zombie
A computer attached to the Internet that has been compromised by a hacker, a computer virus, or a Trojan horse.

"Risk comes from not knowing what you're doing."
Warren Buffet

Index